THE Sasha Kagan

SWEATER BOOK

THE *Sasha Kagan* SWEATER BOOK

DORLING KINDERSLEY LONDON

CONTENTS

Editor Bridget Harris
Art Editor Michele Walker
Designer Polly Dawes
Managing Editor Amy Carroll

First published in Great Britain in 1984
by Dorling Kindersley Limited,
9 Henrietta Street, London WC2E 8PS

British Library Cataloguing in Publication Data
Kagan, Sasha
    The Sasha Kagan sweater book.
    1. Sweaters   2. Knitting – Patterns
    I. Title
    646.4′54   TT825
    ISBN 0-86318-051-5

Printed in Italy by A. Mondadori, Verona

GEOMETRICS

FLOWERS

ETHNIC

NURSERY

INTRODUCTION

Through **The Sasha Kagan Sweater Book** I would like to share with every enthusiastic knitter the pleasure of making beautiful and carefully designed sweaters which are not only highly fashionable but also works of art.

Handknits are fast becoming a fashion staple and nearly all of us are prepared to spend time and money to find a sweater that is both well-designed and of high quality. Mass-produced machine knits no longer satisfy the majority of fashion conscious individuals and instead we tend to want sweaters that are original and carefully made, reflecting an element of handiwork as well as fashion. Over the past few years knitwear has undergone a complete revolution, but amidst today's trends for vibrant colours, foreign textures and evermore innovative shapes, I have intentionally tried to stand apart, designing sweaters that are not only fashionable, but that will also stand the test of time and warrant the care and attention that goes into producing each of these sweaters. My knowledge as a fashion designer, together with my avid love of knitting, have led me to attempt to produce work that encompasses beauty, style and craftsmanship, and I hope very much that in following the patterns in the book you too will share in the enjoyment of making such garments. A successful design, in my eyes, is one that can be worn year after year and will co-ordinate with whatever is in fashion at the time. More often than not, knitwear is one of the longest-wearing items in our wardrobes. Therefore it should be skillfully designed, well-made and based on shapes and patterns that are attractive, enduring and versatile. In **The Sasha Kagan Sweater Book,** I have put together a selection of what has proved to be the best and most successful of my summer and winter collections over the past few years. I sincerely hope that you will derive as much pleasure from making and wearing them as I have from designing them.

Sasha Kagan

Though trained as a painter, I have worked in knitwear for a long while and draw the inspiration for my patterns from a variety of sources. Many of my geometric and more linear designs come out of my head, and all I have to do to capture the feel and look of such a design in yarn is to draw it out on paper. In my studio I keep a store of hundreds of yarns from which I select the shades for these designs. Once I have an idea of the colours I will use, the design is then transferred to graph paper so that I have a basic block of pattern from which my knitters can work. In order to decide on the final colour schemes I have many swatches knitted up, so that I can see just how the colours affect one another within the design. Once the colours and pattern are set, the graphs are sent to each knitter along with details of the garment to be made and accompanying instructions and samples of the yarns to be used, and this is essentially what I have provided for you to work from in the book. For my more complex and figurative designs, however, I look farther afield. Although I find the rural atmosphere of my surroundings in Wales an ideal environment for perfecting my designs, many of them derive from outside research. Textiles and embroideries from the past have greatly influenced me, and particularly in my early days, visits to the Victoria and Albert Museum and the Museum of Mankind in London triggered a multitude of ideas. Nostalgia, too, is a predominant influence on my work. Many of my more figurative patterns are of 1930s and 1940s origin. I try to adapt stitchcraft

Top and above, my studio and pinboard where I gather together ideas. *Left,* a selection of the old patterns which inspire many of my designs. *Right,* pattern charts in the making.

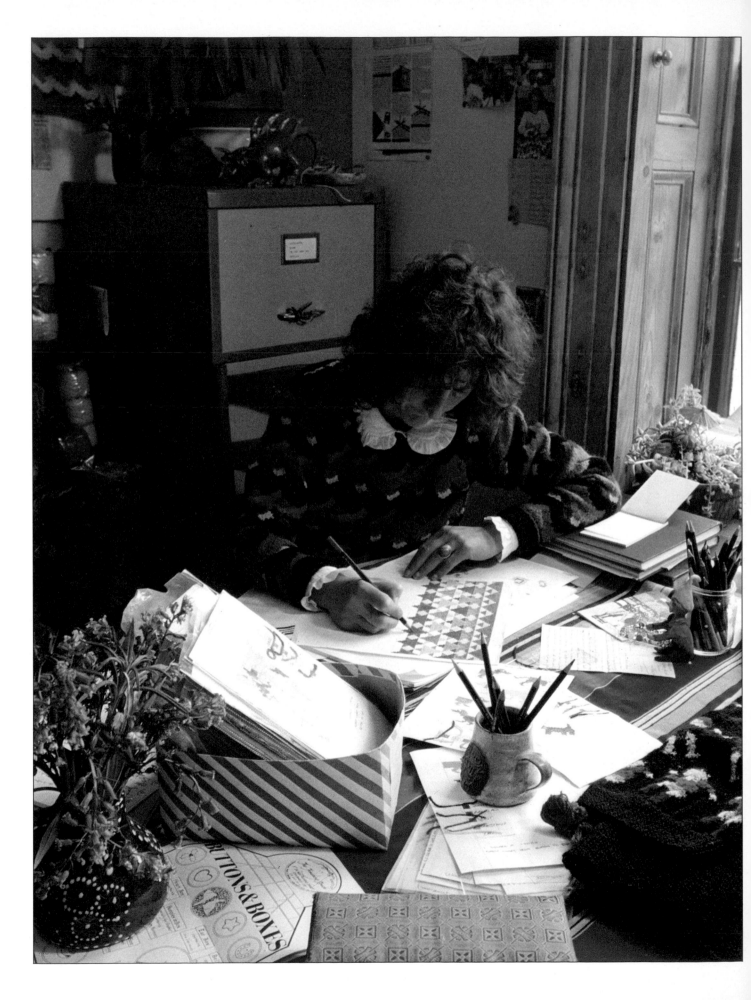

designs such as embroidery motifs, petit point outlines and borders into knitting pattern formulae and use them to form the basis of many of my nursery and flower patterns. To do this, I translate the embroidery stitches into knitting stitches and then work them into a complete design which fits the proportions of a particular choice of sweater. I have a hoard of knitting patterns from the past which I inherited from my mother, and these provide a constant source of ideas for both the patterns and shapes that I use for my work.

While I tend not to design with a specific person or market in mind, I quite often derive ideas for my patterns from a particular climate, season or geographical area. My Cactus motif on pp. 62–63 is associated with a summer spent in south-western America. Normally a season's collection is constructed around a common theme – one year it might be geometrics, another it might be butterflies and birds, another it might be flowers or nursery images – and each collection is characterised by a particular range of colours.

Customers have said that my designs succeed to a great extent on their clever use of colour, however, my criteria for choosing colours are little more than personal taste and trial and error. It is only through having the swatches made that I can see how the colours are affecting one another. Variety is of the essence in any perennial designer's work and so each season I tend to choose a few basic colours which are typical of that collection. In 1983 I used charcoals, greys and blacks, as in the Scotty dog patterns; in 1984 I have explored paintbox shades; other years I have used all pastels, as in the floral designs. By restricting myself to a few colours, my designs take on a more homogeneous look as a collection and by subtly varying the accent and background shades, I achieve variety but not confusion. What I like to do especially is to put two potentially clashing colours side by side within a design and it is this in particular that lends the versatility to my sweaters. A pale delicate pink may come next to a coarse rust mix; white mohair may blend into a strong oatmeal Shetland. I do not believe in monotones and by incorporating contrasting colours within one design I can appeal to several tastes.

Left, hard at work. *Right,* the same pattern worked in different colourways.

The shapes I prefer are classic, and meant to endure from season to season. In my collections I have chosen to limit myself to a select number of garments which all individually conform to basic proportions within which I can manipulate the patterns. Where a particularly complex design is involved, I make certain the shape into which it will be made is simple so as not to confuse the overall effect. Every collection includes a waistcoat, a long-sleeved sweater and a cardigan. Waistcoats, I feel, are versatile garments and something you could easily make for someone else. They are good garments to start off with as they are quick to make and allow plenty of potential to co-ordinate with other items in your wardrobe. More often than not, I work the backs of waistcoats in striped rib, making them straightforward projects.

Long-sleeved sweaters are designed for warmth, and are therefore made in stronger outdoor colours as a rule. Sometimes the pattern is worked throughout on back, front and sleeves, but where a pattern is very dominant, such as the Double Dutch design, the sleeves are left plain to balance the overall effect. Cardigans are easy to wear and are useful for co-ordinating the rest of one's outfit. A plain dress or skirt worn with one of my cardigans makes a stunning and original outfit.

Whilst the basic outlines continue from year to year, I regularly introduce new details to keep pace with contemporary fashion trends and occasionally add a new shape. Shawl collars on waistcoats, peplum skirts on jackets, and matching hats and berets all add new flavour to existing shapes and enhance particular designs.

Basic shapes: *left*, crew neck sweater; *top*, short cardigan and peplum jacket; *top right*, crew neck sweater with plain sleeves; *right*, waistcoat; *far right*, boat neck sweater. *Above*, a waistcoat back worked in striped rib.

I also try to design my shapes with men in mind as well as women. Scattered throughout the book are several sweaters that are particularly suitable for men and these have been sized up accordingly. Similarly, many of the nostalgic figurative sweaters should appeal to teenagers.

I usually prefer to work in Shetland yarn because it is found in a wide range of shades and because my knitters feel comfortable with it. It is particularly suitable for intricate patterns, and the fineness of the yarn is appropriate for the large amount of weaving in and carrying yarns across the back of the work that my patterns require. Since I am mainly concerned with pattern and colour few of my styles use textured stitches. Occasionally, though, I incorporate mohair, silk, and lurex yarn, when I think this will add to my design. My spring and summer garments tend to be in cotton yarn. When working in cotton, I adjust my colours to be brighter and simpler; the straight outlines which the cotton yarn produces would kill a more intricate design, and therefore I stick to bolder figurative patterns. Most of the yarns used are fine – 2-ply jumper weight Shetland yarn is generally the basis for my wool garments, with bands of mohair to separate certain patterns and flecks of lurex to accentuate others. A 4-ply yarn is used for the cotton garments.

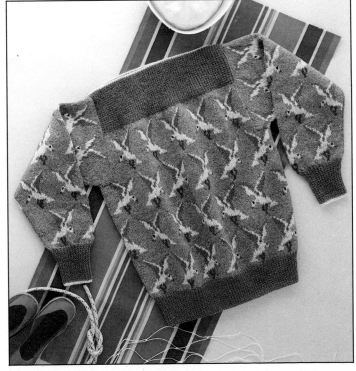

The possibilities for designing your own patterns are endless. At the simplest level, you can follow my designs but substitute colours of your own choice. This can be done by merely changing the shade of a background colour, taking it up or down so that the pattern becomes more or less predominant. Alternatively you can replace one of my background colours with a colour you prefer better. For example, when making the Seagull boat neck sweater on pp. 92–93 you might use a navy blue background in place of the pale background for a stronger effect. When changing a background shade, remember to consider the yarns that are going to be carried across and woven in, taking care that they will not show through the ground colour.

At a slightly more complex level, you can borrow a particular colour scheme from another garment and use it in one of the existing patterns. For example, the colours of the Scotty dog sweaters might appeal to you and you might like to translate these colours into the Prowling Cats crew neck sweater on pp. 102–103, making it more suitable for a man's garment perhaps. When you do this try to make sure that the number of yarns used in both patterns correspond, or decide which ones you can afford to forfeit.

You may find that one of my designs appeals to you but none of my colours tie in with your wardrobe. In this case you could change the colour scheme completely. To do this, first analyse the relationship of one colour to another; does it enhance the colour next to it, does it contrast with it, is it a neutral shade, is it lighter than the next colour or darker. Once you have established this you can then select colours of your choice which will have the same effect within the pattern. You could translate the Dachshund pattern into primary colours against a dark ground, taking them away from their natural colours. Similarly, you can change the colours of the Scotty dog pattern so that you are using the same motif as before but achieving a completely different style. By using a grey ground and less vivid colours you can convert the squares pattern into a much softer design than the bold originals.

These are all examples of using my outlines and patterns to suit your own tastes. But if you are feeling adventurous you might like to try designing your own patterns, translating a motif which appeals or has particular sentimental value into a pattern formula. When I put together a design I have certain maxims I follow, which have evolved largely through trial and error. Just as when building a wall, the bricks should be staggered and not placed directly on top of each other, so it is best to offset your pattern motif as it moves up the work, so that only alternate rows of pattern align. Similarly, if your design has a definite horizontal direction, it is more effective to reverse the direction on alternate rows to give 'movement'

Above, bands of white mohair worked in reversed stocking stitch are used to separate a repeating pattern. *Left,* examples of different backgrounds and colourways of patterns featured in the book.

within the garment. If your ground colour is over-dominant you can introduce horizontal bands or stripes of different plain stitches, such as garter stitch, or different yarns in between the pattern rows, to break up the design quite simply. I have also found that border colours are of great importance and often work in the opposite direction to that which you would expect. They do not always have to be mute, back-up colours; it is sometimes possible to use a strong, perhaps contrasting shade; but experiment with yarns before making your final decision to ensure that you do not kill an otherwise subtle and interesting colour combination within the pattern.

Once you have started thinking in terms of specific patterns and designs – whether they are of mine or your own inspiration – you will find that different designs will develop out of one another. The colours used in a bold figurative design might translate interestingly into a more miniature geometric design and vice versa. Do not be afraid to knit up smallish squares of your pattern incorporating any border design you might have envisaged, to see whether your ideas are effective.

I first trained as a painter at Exeter College of Art and then studied printmaking at the Royal College of Art. I concentrated on prints filled with patterns, and then went on to produce silkscreens based on various knitting stitches. My mother had been a great knitter and hoarder of scraps of yarn and was herself a professional needlewoman. I grew up to believe that knitting in many ways represents the ultimate in endeavour and application, and I feel lucky to have taken up the craft in our increasingly technological age at a time when it is becoming more appreciated and sought after.

I came to live in Wales in 1972 and found its compact ruralness a great advantage when I began to translate the repeat patterns and graphic qualities of prints into knitwear. In 1977 I was awarded a Welsh Arts Council bursary to set up a dye workshop and began organised production of my knitwear designs with four outworkers. Today my knitwear business is thriving; I have a core of around a hundred knitters who come from all over the country, and who produce the 800–1000 garments I now sell commercially in London, Milan, Berlin, New York and San Francisco. Buyers say that my unique designs have international appeal, and that customers appreciate the good finish and hand-made quality that distinguishes my work.

I am greatly indebted to the help and support I receive from the team of workers who contribute to the beautiful finish and commercial success of my sweaters. I would especially like to thank the following people for their industry: Marlene Richards for finishing the sweaters, Mrs M. Jones and Mrs E. Holmes for working pattern swatches and Maria Feltham for organising the production of the sweaters and co-ordinating sending the yarns and patterns to the knitters. Most of all, the business would not be the thriving concern it is today without the help and support of my husband, Robert, who has been my business partner over the last 10 years, and who travels the world selling my sweaters and promoting the business.

Above right, drawing charts for my knitters; *right,* choosing yarns to be sent off. *Top far right,* with my family; *below far right,* working out pattern swatches.

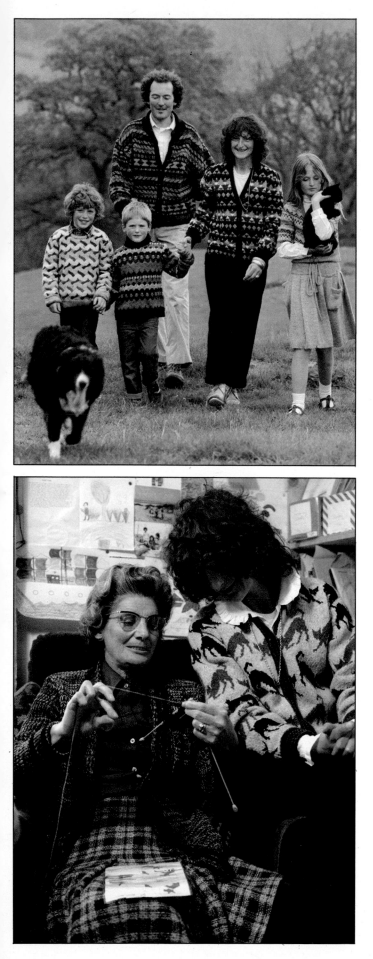

Individual patterns are given for each of the sweaters illustrated in the book, and these, along with the appropriate pattern charts, are found beside each photograph. However, I strongly advise those of you who are new to knitting patterns from charts to consult the Knitting Know-how section at the back of the book. There you will find a detailed breakdown of how these particular charts and patterns should be read when making the sweaters (see pp. 134–135). Also at the back of the book are a list of abbreviations, and illustrated step by step instructions for all the stitches you will require. The majority of the patterns are given in several sizes where the design permits, and the sizes are quoted at the beginning of each pattern. A breakdown of the measurements corresponding to these sizes is given on pp. 116–123, along with sketches of each of the sweaters, to give a better idea of the proportions of each garment. These measurements and the measurements quoted within the pattern are calculated as though perfect tension had been maintained throughout. Instructions about working the yarns in the patterns given in the book, about maintaining and adjusting tension, and working the yarns to correspond with the pattern charts provided are given fully in the back of the book on pp. 136–137. I further advise you to consult these pages if this method of knitting is new to you. Obviously, if your tension is not exact and you decide to shape the piece you are working on a different row from that quoted, your pattern will not correspond with the photograph in the book. When several sizes are quoted, the measurements, yarn quantities and numbers of stitches for the larger sizes are quoted in brackets after the initial figure.

Many of the garments have been designed with a unisex element in mind. In those patterns I have given instructions for working right over left opening edges on cardigans and waistcoats. However, if you wish to make the garments for a man, these can easily be reversed.

Making up instructions are given at the end of each pattern, but fuller, illustrated instructions are given on pp. 140–141 in the Knitting Know-how section. For yarn suppliers and manufacturers see pp. 142–143. Alongside the measurements charts on pp. 116–123 there are samples of the yarns which I have used, to help give you a better idea of the colours. Quantities of yarn quoted in the patterns are generally the minimum amounts required, and they are given in multiples of the quantities in which they can be bought. In some cases, however, only very small quantities of a shade are required, perhaps for working eyes or specks of pattern. For these you can use scraps of yarn if you have them, so study the pattern before you buy your own. Always bear in mind that the way in which you work the patterns and join in colours will affect the yarn quantities.

GEOMETRICS

HARRIET

*A warm three-quarter length jacket for cold days,
with striped rib double borders and slit hip pockets.*

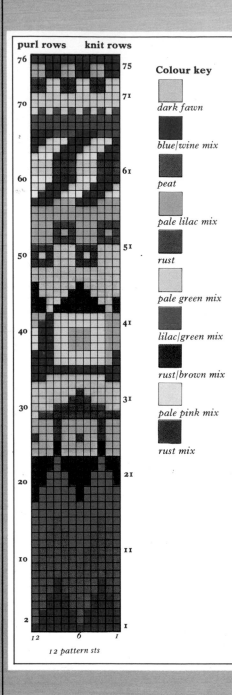

purl rows	knit rows	

Colour key

dark fawn

blue/wine mix

peat

pale lilac mix

rust

pale green mix

lilac/green mix

rust/brown mix

pale pink mix

rust mix

12 pattern sts

MATERIALS

Yarn
Use 2-ply jumper weight Shetland yarn.
Yarn A 175g *(dark fawn)*
Yarn B 75g *(blue/wine mix)*
Yarn C 75g *(peat)*
Yarn D 75g *(pale lilac mix)*
Yarn E 75g *(rust)*
Yarn F 75g *(pale green mix)*
Yarn G 50g *(lilac/green mix)*
Yarn H 50g *(rust/blue mix)*
Yarn J 25g *(pale pink mix)*
Yarn K 25g *(rust mix)*

Needles

1 pair size 3¼mm
1 pair size 3mm
1 pair size 2¾mm
Notions
8 buttons

MEASUREMENTS

To fit chest 91 (97)cm (36, 38in).
(See also chart on p. 116.)
Tension
32 sts and 32 rows measure 10cm over
Fair Isle pattern on 3¼mm needles.

BACK

With 2¾mm needles and yarn A, cast on
142 (154) sts. **Work 18cm in k1, p1
twisted rib in the following colours:
Row 1: Yarn C
Row 2: Yarn E
Row 3: Yarn A
Repeat rows 1–3 for 18cm, ending with a
row in yarn A**. Increase across the next
(wrong-side) row as follows: (yarn C) rib 1
(7) sts, *rib 6 sts, rib twice into next st;
repeat from * 19 more times, rib 1 (7) sts –
162 (174) sts.
Change to 3¼mm needles and st st and
work Fair Isle pattern from chart, reading
odd (knit) rows from right to left and even
(purl) rows from left to right. Work the
pattern across knit rows as follows: *for the
smaller size* (91cm), repeat sts 1–12
thirteen times and then work sts 1–6 once
to complete row; *for the larger size* (97cm),
repeat sts 1–12 fourteen times and then
work sts 1–6 once. Work purl rows in
reverse. Continuing in pattern, work
straight until you have completed row 64
of the second working of chart and back
measures approximately 62cm.
Shape armholes: Continuing in pattern,
cast off 10 (12) sts at the beginning of the
next 2 rows – 142 (150) sts **remain**. Work
straight until end of row 62 **(66)** of third
working of chart and **back measures**
approximately 84 (85)cm.
Shape shoulders: Continuing in pattern,
cast off 11 (12) sts at the beginning of next
8 rows. Cast off remaining 54 (54) sts.

FRONTS

Left front
***With 2¾mm needles and yarn A, cast
on 64 (68) sts. Work as for back from ** to
**. Increase on next (wrong-side) row as
follows: (yarn C) rib 0 (4) sts, *rib 7 (5)
sts, rib twice into next st; repeat from * 7
(9) more times, rib 0 (4) sts – 72 (78) sts.
Change to 3¼mm needles and st st and
work pattern from chart. Work the pattern
across knit rows as follows: *for the smaller
size*, repeat sts 1–12 six times; *for the
larger size*, repeat sts 1–12 six times, then

work sts 1–6. Work purl rows in reverse.
Continue in pattern to end of row 22 (24)
of the chart.***
Pocket: Work pocket over the next 32
rows as follows: on the next row, work the
first 32 (38) sts in the row, turn, leaving
the remaining 40 sts on a spare needle.
Work the next 31 rows of the pattern on
these first 32 (38) sts – you should have
completed row 54 (56) of the chart. Then
leave these 32 (38) sts on a spare needle.
With right side facing, return to the 40 sts
on the other spare needle and work the
same 32 rows of pattern on these sts
ending at row 54 (56) of the chart. Now
slip both sets of stitches on to one needle
and continue to work straight in pattern
until end of row 64 of the second working
of chart and front measures approximately
62cm.
Shape armhole: Continuing in pattern,
cast off 10 (12) sts at the beginning of next
row – 62 (66) sts remain. Work straight
until end of row 39 (43) of the third working of chart.
Shape neck: Cast off 5 sts at the beginning of the next (wrong-side) row, then
work pattern to end. Continue in pattern,
decreasing one st at the neck edge on the
following 13 rows – 44 (48) sts remain.
Now work straight until end of row 62
(66) of the third working of chart and
front measures approximately 84 (85)cm.
Shape shoulder: Cast off 11 (12) sts at
the beginning of the next and following 3
alternate rows.

Right front

Work as for left front, reversing pocket,
armhole, neck and shoulder shapings.
When working the pocket, work the first
40 sts in the row (right-side facing) and
then work the remaining 32 sts.

SLEEVES

With 2¾mm needles and yarn A, cast
on 68 (70) sts. Work 20cm in striped
rib as for back. Increase across last
row as follows: rib 2 (5) sts, *rib 3 (2)
sts, rib twice into next st; repeat from
* 15 (19) more times, rib 2 (5) sts –
84 (90) sts.
Change to 3¼mm needles and st st and
work Fair Isle pattern from chart.
Work pattern across knit rows as
follows: *for the smaller size*, repeat sts
1–12 seven times; *for the larger size*,
repeat sts 1–12 seven times and then
work sts 1–6 once to complete the row.
Work purl rows in reverse. Continue
in pattern, *at the same time* increasing
one st at each end of the 3rd and every
following 4th row until there are 144
(150) sts on needle. Work straight until
end of row 48 of second working of chart
and sleeve measures 58cm. Cast off.

FRONT BORDERS

Measure 9cm up from edge of hem welt at front opening edges and mark points.

Right front

With right side facing, using 2¾mm needles and yarn A, pick up and knit 216 (220) sts up front opening edge from marker to start of neck shaping. Work 5 rows in twisted rib in the same three-colour stripe sequence as for back welts.

Buttonholes: Make 8 buttonholes in the 6th row as follows: rib 6 (7) sts, *cast off 4 sts, rib 25 sts; rep from * 6 more times, cast off 4 sts, rib 3 (6) sts. Rib back along next row, casting on 4 sts over those cast off in previous row. Rib 8 more rows, then work the two buttonhole rows again. Work 5 more rows of rib; cast off.

Left front

With right side facing, 2¼mm needles and yarn A, beginning at start of neck shaping, pick up and knit 216 (220) sts down front edge to marker. Work 22 rows of rib to correspond with right front band, omit buttonholes. Cast off.

COLLAR

With 2¾mm needles and yarn A, cast on 116 (118) sts. Work one row in rib in yarn A. Using same colour sequence as before, work collar in striped rib, increasing one st at each end of next and following 5 alternate rows. Then increase one st at each end of the next 6 rows – 140 (142) sts. Continuing in rib, work 4 rows straight then decrease one st at each end of the next 6 rows, then decrease one st at each end of next and following five alternate rows – 116 (118) sts. Work one row straight. Cast off.

POCKET

Pocket borders

Left front: With 2¾mm needles and yarn A, and with right side facing, pick up and knit 34 sts up the side of the pocket slit nearest the front opening edge. Work 12 rows of striped k1, p1 twisted rib, as before. Cast off.

Right front: Work in same way, beginning at opposite end of pocket slit.

Pocket linings

With right side facing, using 3mm needles and yarn A, pick up and knit 34 sts down the remaining edge of one pocket slit, behind ribbed border. Work 13cm in st st in yarn A; cast off. Repeat for other pocket.

TO MAKE UP

Press all pieces from the wrong side avoiding ribbing. Join fronts to back at side and shoulder seams. Join sleeve seams, leaving 3 (4)cm unstitched at top of seam. Sew sleeves and collar in position in same way as Leaves cardigan (see p. 81). Fold cuff ribbings in half to inside and slip stitch inner edges in position inside sleeves. Fold front ribbed bands in half to inside, aligning double buttonholes in right front band. Slip stitch inner edge of bands in position down inside front edges and blanket stitch around double buttonholes. Fold up half of hem welt to inside and pin inner edge in position. Slip stitch to main body of garment, oversewing the double edges at front opening edges. Sew free sides of each pocket lining to back of cardigan fronts. Catch down sides of pocket borders. Sew 8 buttons to left front band to match buttonholes. Press seams from wrong side.

DESERT RIBBONS

A short cardigan with three-quarter sleeves and front pockets,
worked in subtle desert shades of ribbon pattern.
It could easily be made in bolder shades for a livelier effect.

MATERIALS

Yarn

Use 2-ply jumper weight Shetland yarn.
Yarn A 125g *(sand)*
Yarn B 125g *(ivory)*
Yarn C 75g *(pale lilac mix)*
Yarn D 50g *(mid-brown mix)*
Yarn E 25g *(pearl)*
Yarn F 25g *(sage green)*

Needles

1 pair size 3¼mm
1 pair size 3mm
1 pair size 2¾mm

Notions

5 buttons

MEASUREMENTS

One-size: to fit bust 86–91cm (34–36in).
(See also chart on p. 116.)

Tension

30 sts and 32 rows measure 10cm over
Fair Isle pattern on 3¼mm needles.

BACK

With 2¾mm needles and yarn A, cast on
128 sts. Work 5cm in k1, p1 twisted rib,
increasing across the last (wrong-side) row
as follows: *rib 7 sts, rib twice into the
next st; repeat from * 16 more times –
144 sts.

Change to 3¼mm needles and st st and
work Fair Isle pattern from chart, reading
odd (knit) rows from right to left and even
(purl) rows from left to right. Work the
pattern across knit rows as follows: work
sts *10–17* once at the beginning of the row
and then repeat the 17 pattern sts (*1–17*)
eight times across the row. Work purl
rows in reverse, working extra sts at the
end of rows. Continuing in pattern work
sides straight until you have worked row
18 of the third working of the pattern
chart and the back measures approximately 28cm from the cast-on edge.

Shape armholes: Continuing in pattern,
cast off 8 sts at the beginning of the next 2
rows. Then decrease one st at each end of
every row until 108 sts remain. Work
straight in pattern on these 108 sts until
you have worked row 28 of the fifth working of the pattern chart and back measures
approximately 49cm from cast-on edge.

Shape shoulders: Continuing in pattern,
cast off 6 sts at the beginning of the next 4
rows. Then cast off 7 sts at the beginning
of the following 6 rows. Divide the
remaining 42 sts in half and leave each
half on a spare needle or stitch holder.

FRONTS

Pocket linings

Begin by making the pocket linings. With 3mm needles and yarn A, cast on 28 sts. Work 6cm in st st in yarn A, ending with a purl row. Leave sts on spare needle. Make another lining in the same way.

Left front

With 2¾mm needles and yarn A, cast on 58 sts. Work 5cm in k1, p1 twisted rib in yarn A, increasing across the last wrong-side row as follows: *rib 6 sts, rib twice into the next st; repeat from * 7 more times, rib 2 sts – 66 sts.

Change to 3¼mm needles and st st and work Fair Isle pattern from chart, working the pattern across knit rows as follows: repeat sts 1–17, three times and then work sts 1–15 once to complete the row. Work purl rows in reverse, working sts 15–1 at the beginning of the row. Continuing in pattern, work straight until you have completed row 14 of the chart.

Pocket: Introduce pocket in row 15 as follows: work the pattern across the first 19 sts in the row, then slip the next 28 sts on to a spare needle or stitch holder and in their place work the pattern across the 28 sts of one pocket lining on spare needle, then work the pattern to the end of the row. Continuing in pattern, work straight until you have worked row 18 of the third working of the pattern chart and the front measures approximately 28cm from the cast-on edge.

Shape armhole and neck edge: Continuing in pattern, cast off 8 sts at the beginning of the next row and then work the pattern to the last 2 sts in row; k2 tog. K2 tog at the armhole edge on the next 10 rows and then work armhole edge straight. *At the same time,* continue to decrease one st at the neck edge on every following 4th

row after the first decrease on row 19 until 33 sts remain. Then work straight until you have worked row 28 of the fifth working of the pattern chart and front measures approximately 49cm from the cast-on edge.

Shape shoulder: Continuing in pattern, cast off 6 sts at the beginning of the next and following alternate row. Then cast off 7 sts at the beginning of the next and following 2 alternate rows.

Right front

Work as for left front, but reverse pocket, armhole, neck and shoulder shapings.

SLEEVES

With 2¾mm needles and yarn D, cast on 62 sts. Work one row in k1, p1 twisted rib in yarn D. Join in yarn A and work a further 8cm in k1, p1 twisted rib in yarn A, increasing across the last (wrong-side) row as follows: rib 11 sts, *rib twice into the next st; repeat from * 39 more times, rib 11 sts – 102 sts.

Change to 3¼mm needles and st st and work Fair Isle pattern from chart, repeating sts 1–17, six times across knit rows, and working purl rows in reverse. Continuing in pattern, work sleeve straight until you have completed row 18 of the third working of the pattern chart and the sleeve measures approximately 31cm from the cast-on edge.

Shape top of sleeve: Continuing in pattern, cast off 8 sts at the beginning of the next 2 rows. K2 tog at each end of the

next and following alternate row, nine times in all. You should now have completed row 11 of the fourth working of the pattern chart. Then work 24 rows straight, ending on row 7 of the fifth working of the pattern chart. K2 tog at each end of the next and every following alternate row, six times, then k2 tog at each end of every row, ten times. Cast off the remaining sts. This wide sleeve top will then be pleated into the armhole.

Make another sleeve in the same way.

Join fronts to back at shoulder seams.

FRONT BANDS

Right front

With right side of work facing, using 2¾mm needles and yarn A, beginning at the lower edge, pick up and knit 93 sts up the front opening edge to the start of the neck shaping; then pick up 92 sts around side of neck to centre-back, including the 21 sts on the first spare needle – 185 sts. Work 3 rows in twisted rib in yarn A.

Buttonholes: Make 5 buttonholes in the 4th row of ribbing as follows: rib 4 sts, *cast off 3 sts, rib 18 sts; repeat from * 3 more times, cast off 3 sts, rib to end of row. On the next row (row 5 of ribbing) work back in rib, casting on 3 sts directly over those cast off in previous row. Work 4 more rows in rib in yarn A. Join in yarn D and work one row of rib in yarn D. Cast off in rib in yarn D.

Left front

With 2¾mm needles and yarn A, and with right side of work facing, knit the 21 sts from the remaining spare needle, then continue to pick up and knit 71 sts around neck to start of neck shaping, then pick up and knit a further 93 sts down front opening to lower edge – 185 sts in all. Work to correspond with right front band, omitting buttonholes.

POCKET TOPS

With 2¾mm needles and yarn A, rib across the 28 sts of one pocket on spare needle. Work 7 more rows in k1, p1 twisted rib in yarn A. Join in yarn D and work a further row in twisted rib in yarn D. Cast off in rib in yarn D. Repeat for other pocket top.

TO MAKE UP

Press all Fair Isle parts lightly from the wrong side, avoiding ribbing. Join fronts to back at side seams. Join underarm sleeve seams. Pin sleeves into each armhole, pleating the fullness around the top of the sleeve as you pin in position. Sew sleeves into armholes. Join front bands at centre-back of neck. Sew down sides of each pocket top and sew around the sides of each pocket lining on wrong side. Sew on 5 buttons to correspond with buttonholes. Press seams lightly from wrong side.

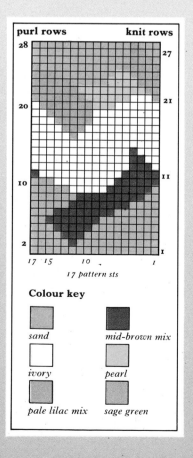

purl rows   knit rows

28   27

20   21

10   11

2   1

17 15   10   1

17 pattern sts

Colour key

sand   *mid-brown mix*

ivory   *pearl*

pale lilac mix   *sage green*

MATERIALS Hat

Yarn
Use 2-ply jumper-weight Shetland yarn unless otherwise indicated.
Yarn A 50g *(black)*
Yarn B 50g lurex *(copper)*
Yarn C 25g *(rust)*
Yarn D 25g *(peat)*
Yarn E 50g *(wine)*

Needles
1 pair size 3¼mm (long or circular)
1 pair size 2¾mm (long or circular)

MEASUREMENTS
One-size: to fit an average head.
(See also chart on p. 116.)

Tension
32 sts and 32 rows measure 10cm over Fair Isle pattern on 3¼mm needles.

OPTICAL COPPER

*Matching waistcoat and hat in dark shades with glints of copper
scattered throughout. The copper yarn could, however, be substituted
for a Shetland yarn to give a more subtle effect.*

Headband

With 2¾mm needles and yarn A, cast on
160 sts. Work in k1, p1 twisted rib in the
following three-colour sequence:
Row 1: Yarn E
Row 2: Yarn B
Row 3: Yarn A
Repeat rows 1–3 until the band measures
approximately 11cm, ending with a row in
yarn A. Increase for crown on the next
wrong-side row as follows: (yarn E), *p1,
purl into front and back of next st; repeat
from * to end – 240 sts.
Change to 3¼mm needles and st st and
work Fair Isle pattern from chart reading
odd (knit) rows from right to left and even
(purl) rows from left to right. Repeat the
16 pattern sts, fifteen times across the
rows. Work rows 1 to 54 on chart.
Shape crown: With right side facing and
continuing in st st, work in stripes,
decreasing as follows:
Row 1 (Yarn E) *k8, slip 1, k1, pass
slipped stitch over (psso); repeat from *
to end – 216 sts.
Purl one row (yarn B), knit one row
(yarn A).
Row 4 (Yarn E) *p7, slip 1, p1, psso;
repeat from * to end – 192 sts.
Knit one row (yarn B), purl one row
(yarn A).
Row 7 (Yarn E) *k6, slip 1, k1, psso;
repeat from * to end – 168 sts.
Purl one row (yarn B), knit one row
(yarn A).
Row 10 (Yarn E) *p5, slip 1, p1, psso;
repeat from * to end – 144 sts.
Then knit one row (yarn B), purl one row
(yarn A). Continue thus, working a
decrease row on every 3rd row (i.e.
decreasing 24 sts on every decrease row)
until you have worked the row *p1, slip 1,
p1, psso; repeat from * to end – 48 sts.
**Knit one row, purl one row. Next row,
k2 tog to end of row. Repeat from ** once
more. Work 2 rows straight – 6 sts. Break
yarn leaving 15cm end. Thread end of
yarn through remaining 6 sts, draw up
and secure.

TO MAKE UP

Press Fair Isle parts lightly from wrong
side. Join seam from crown to edge of
headband, with 15cm length of yarn. Fold
headband in half, turning it in to wrong
side. Pin and slip stitch in place all round.

MATERIALS Waistcoat

Yarn
Yarn A 125 (150, 150)g *(black)*
Yarn B 75g lurex *(copper)*
Yarn C 25g *(rust)*
Yarn D 25g *(peat)*
Yarn E 50g *(wine)*
Needles
1 pair size 3¼ mm
1 pair size 3mm
1 pair size 2¾mm
Notions
5 buttons

MEASUREMENTS

To fit bust 84 (91, 99)cm (33, 36, 39in).
Tension
32 sts and 32 rows measure 10cm over
Fair Isle pattern on 3¼mm needles.

FRONT

Pocket linings
Begin by making pocket linings as
follows: with 3mm needles and yarn A,
cast on 28 (32, 36) sts. Work 7cm in st st
in yarn A, ending with a purl row. Transfer the sts to a spare needle or stitch
holder. Make another pocket lining in the
same way.

Left front
**With 2¾mm needles and yarn A, cast on
66 (72, 78) sts. Work in k1, p1 twisted rib
in following three-colour stripe sequence:
Row 1: Yarn E
Row 2: Yarn B
Row 3: Yarn A
Repeat rows 1–3 until the work measures
5cm, ending on a wrong-side row**.
Change to 3¼mm needles and st st and
work Fair Isle pattern from chart, reading
odd (knit) rows from right to left and even
(purl) rows from left to right. Work the
pattern across knit rows as follows: repeat
sts (1–16) four times *for all sizes* and then
work sts 1–2 *for the small size*; sts 1–8 *for
the medium size* and sts 1–14 *for the large
size,* to complete the row. Work purl rows
in reverse. Continue in pattern until end
of row 20.

Colour key

black

copper

rust

peat

wine

continued on p. 31

RIB & BRAMBLE

*Two plain garments based on 1930s shapes. The Rib sweater is close-fitting
with diagonal ribs moving outwards from a central panel.
The Bramble sweater has puff and darted sleeves.*

RIBBONS

*A loose-fitting long-sleeved winter sweater with a wide
boat neck and dropped shoulders. The matching pixie hat uses bands
of the same pattern, worked between a black background.*

MATERIALS Hat

Yarn
Use 2-ply jumper weight Shetland yarn.
Yarn A 75g *(black)*
Yarn B 25g *(mustard)*
Yarn C 25g *(green)*
Yarn D 25g *(bright blue)*
Yarn E 25g *(red)*
Yarn F 25g *(peat)*

Needles
1 set of four *or* circular, size 3¼mm
1 set of four *or* circular, size 3mm
1 set of four *or* circular, size 2¾mm

MEASUREMENTS

One-size: to fit an average head.
(See also chart on p. 117.)

Tension
32 sts and 30 rows measure 10cm over
Fair Isle pattern on 3¼mm needles.

Headband
With the set of 2¾mm needles or circular
2¾mm needle, and yarn A, cast on 154 sts
(i.e. 51 sts on each of 2 needles and 52 sts
on the third needle). Work 15cm in k1, p1
twisted rib in rounds, decreasing one st at
the end of the last round – 153 sts.
Shape crown: Change to 3¼mm needles
and work pattern from chart. Because you
are working in rounds, read all rows from
right to left and knit every row. Repeat the
17 pattern sts on chart nine times around.
Work rows 1–28 of pattern chart twice.
On the next round, knit entire round in
yarn A, increasing 3 sts evenly – 156 sts.
Change to 3mm needles and continue in
yarn A only, decreasing to a point as
follows:
1st decrease round: (K10, k2 tog) 13
times. Knit 19 rounds straight.
2nd decrease round: (K9, k2 tog) 13
times. Knit 19 rounds straight.
3rd decrease round: (K8, k2 tog) 13
times. Knit 19 rounds straight.
4th decrease round: (K7, k2 tog) 13
times. Knit 19 rounds straight.
Continue decreasing in this way, working
one decrease round and then 19 rounds
straight until you have worked the round
(k1, k2 tog) 13 times – 26 sts remain.
Knit a further 19 rounds straight.
Then (k2 tog) 13 times. Knit 6 rounds
straight. Break yarn leaving a 13cm end.

TO MAKE UP

Thread the yarn end through the remaining sts on the needle and draw up tightly.
Secure end and darn in. Make a pom-pom
from the remaining yarns and sew on to
end of hat. Press lightly from wrong side,
avoiding ribbing.

MATERIALS Jumper

Yarn
Use 2-ply jumper weight Shetland yarn.
Yarn A 150g *(peat)*
Yarn B 75g *(black)*
Yarn C 50g *(red)*
Yarn D 50g *(green)*
Yarn E 25g *(bright blue)*
Yarn F 25g *(mustard)*

Needles
1 pair size 3¼mm
1 pair size 2¼mm

MEASUREMENTS

To fit chest 91 (97)cm (36, 38in).
(See also chart on p. 117.)

Tension
31 sts and 30 rows measure 10cm over
Fair Isle pattern on 3¼mm needles.

BACK and FRONT

With 2¼mm needles and yarn A, cast on
128 (136) sts. Work 5cm in k1, p1 twisted
rib, increasing across the last wrong-side
row as follows: *rib 3 sts, rib twice into
the next st, rib 4 sts; repeat from * 15 (16)
more times – 144 (153) sts.
Change to 3¼mm needles and st st and
work pattern from chart, reading odd
(knit) rows from right to left and even
(purl) rows from left to right. Work the
pattern across knit rows as follows: *for the
smaller size,* repeat sts *1–17* eight times,
then work sts *1–8* once to complete row;
for the larger size, work sts *1–17* nine
times across the rows. Work purl rows in
reverse. Continue thus in pattern until
you have worked row 12 (16) of the fourth
working of the pattern chart and the work
measures approximately 37 (38)cm from
the cast-on edge.
Shape armholes: Continuing in pattern,
cast off 10 (12) sts at the beginning of the
next 2 rows – 124 (129) sts. Then work
straight in pattern until you have completed row 24 (28) of the fifth working of
the pattern chart and the work measures
approximately 50 (51)cm from the cast-
on edge.
Change to 2¼mm needles and with yarn A
only work 10 (11)cm in k1, p1 twisted rib
to form boat neck, increasing one st at
each end of the first row, *for the larger
size only.* When you have worked 10
(11)cm, join in yarn B and work a further
row of rib in yarn B. Cast off in rib in
yarn B.
Make another in the same way for front.

SLEEVES

With 2¼mm needles and yarn B, cast on
60 sts. Work one row in k1, p1 twisted rib
in yarn B. Change to yarn A and work 8

(9)cm in twisted rib, increasing across the
last wrong-side row as follows: rib 5 sts,
*rib 2 sts, rib twice into the next st;
repeat from * 15 more times, rib 7 sts
– 76 sts.
Change to 3¼mm needles and st st and
work Fair Isle pattern from chart, repeating
sts *1–17* four times and then working sts
1–8 once across knit rows. Work purl rows
in reverse. Continuing in pattern, shape
the sides by increasing one st at each end
of the 7th and every following 4th row
until there are 132 (136) sts on the needle.
Take the extra sts into the pattern as they
are made. Then work straight in pattern
until you have worked row 24 (28) of the
fifth working of the chart and the sleeve
measures approximately 53 (55)cm from
the cast-on edge. Cast off right across.

SWEATER
Colour key

purl rows · knit rows

peat

black

red

green

bright blue

mustard

17 pattern sts

knit rows · **HAT**
Colour key

peat

black

red

green

bright blue

mustard

17 pattern sts

TO MAKE UP

Press all pieces lightly from the wrong side, avoiding ribbing. Join front to back at side seams. Overlap the front half of the boat neck and the back half by 2cm and hold with a pin. Sew front of boat neck to back of boat neck from shoulder edge to point 5cm in, lifting the front welt and catching down the underneath to the back welt so stitches are invisible. Join sleeve seams, leaving the last 4cm at top of seam unstitched. Pin straight cast-off edge at top of sleeve into top of armhole and pin either side of the unstitched sleeve seam across straight cast-off edge at bottom of armhole. Sew in place. Repeat for other sleeve. Then press seams lightly.

CHEQUER·BOARD

*Chequered squares of pattern in a mixture of shades
make this warm wool sweater suitable for both men and women.
It has a crew neck and slightly dropped shoulders.*

MATERIALS

Yarn
Use 2-ply jumper weight Shetland yarn.
Yarn A 125 (150)g *(oat)*
Yarn B 75 (100)g *(ivory)*
Yarn C 75 (100)g *(dark fawn)*
Yarn D 50g *(rust)*
Yarn E 50g *(lilac/green mix)*
Yarn F 25g *(clan green)*
Yarn G 25g *(bottle green)*
Yarn H 25g *(purple)*
Yarn J 25g *(peat)*

Needles
1 pair size 3¼mm
1 pair size 2¾mm
1 circular needle, size 2¾mm

MEASUREMENTS
To fit chest 91–97 (102–107)cm (36–38,
40–42in).
(See also chart on p. 117.)

Tension
32 sts and 30 rows measure 10cm over
Fair Isle pattern on 3¼mm needles.

BACK

**With 2¾mm needles and yarn A, cast on 136 (150) sts. Work 5 (6)cm in k1, p1 twisted rib, increasing on the last (wrong-side) row as follows: rib 2 (3) sts, *rib 6 (5) sts, rib twice into next st; repeat from * 17 (23) more times, rib 8 (3) sts – 154 (174) sts in all.

Change to 3¼mm needles and work pattern from chart, reading odd (knit) rows from right to left and even (purl) rows from left to right. Repeat the basic 10 pattern sts (*1–10*) fifteen (seventeen) times and work the extra 4 sts (*11–14*) indicated at the end of knit rows and at the beginning of purl rows. Continuing in pattern, work straight until you have worked the 30 rows of the pattern chart four times and the back measures approximately 45 (46)cm from the cast-on edge.

Shape armholes: Continuing in pattern, cast off 12 (15) sts at the beginning of the next 2 rows (rows 1 and 2 of fifth working of the pattern chart) – 130 (144) sts.**

Continuing in pattern work straight until you have worked row 10 (14) of the seventh working of the pattern chart and armhole measures 23 (24)cm from start of armhole shaping.

Shape shoulders: Continuing in pattern, cast off 15 (17) sts at the beginning of the next 2 rows. Then cast off 13 (14) sts at the beginning of the next 4 rows. Transfer the remaining 48 (54) sts to a spare needle or stitch holder.

FRONT

Work front as for back from ** to ** – 130 (144) sts. Continuing in pattern work straight until you have worked row 8 of the sixth working of the pattern chart and front measures approximately 57 (58)cm from cast-on edge.

Shape neck: Continuing in pattern, on the next row, work the first 47 (53) sts of the row and slip these 47 (53) sts on to a spare needle or stitch holder; cast off the next 36 (38) sts in the row, then work the remaining 47 (53) sts in pattern. Continue in pattern on these last 47 (53) sts, decreasing one st at the neck edge on the next 6 rows – 41 (47) sts. Then work these 41 (47) sts straight in pattern until you have worked row 10 (14) of the sixth working of the pattern chart and right front measures approximately 23 (24)cm from start of armhole shaping.

Shape shoulder: Continuing in pattern cast off 15 (17) sts at the beginning of the next row. Then cast off 13 (14) sts at the beginning of the 2 alternate rows.

With wrong side of the work facing, rejoin yarn to the first 47 (53) sts at the neck edge. Work left shoulder and neck shaping to match right side, reversing all shapings.

SLEEVES

With 2¾mm needles and yarn D, cast on 60 (68) sts and work one row in k1, p1 twisted rib in yarn D. Join in yarn A and work a further 10cm in twisted rib in yarn A, increasing on the last wrong-side row as follows: rib 0 (1), *rib 7 (5) sts, rib twice into the next st, rib 7 (5) sts; repeat from * 3 (5) more times, rib 0 (1) – 64 (74) sts in all.

Change to 3¼mm needles and work Fair Isle pattern from chart, repeating sts *1–10* six (seven) times across the row and working the extra 4 sts (*11–14*) indicated at the end of knit rows and at the beginning of purl rows. Shape sides of sleeve by increasing one st at each end of the 3rd and every following 4th row, until there are 106 (116) sts on the needle, taking the extra sts into the pattern as they are made. Then increase one st at each end of every 3rd row until there are 142 (148) sts on the needle. Continuing in pattern, work straight until you have worked row 16 (24) of the fifth working of the pattern chart and the sleeve measures approximately 55 (58)cm from cast-on edge. Cast off fairly loosely across row – this cast-off edge should measure 47 (48)cm to fit around armhole. Make another sleeve in the same way.

NECKBAND

Join front to back at shoulders. Using the circular 2¾mm needle and yarn A, beginning at the left shoulder seam, pick up and knit 39 (43) sts down left side of neck, then 36 (38) sts across front cast-off edge, 39 (43) sts up the right side of the neck, and finally the 48 (54) sts on the spare needle at the back – 160 (178) sts altogether. Work 10 rounds in twisted rib in yarn A. Join in yarn D and work one round in rib in yarn D. Cast off in rib in yarn D.

TO MAKE UP

Press all pieces lightly from the wrong side, avoiding ribbing. Join front to back at side seams. Join underarm sleeve seams, leaving 4 (5)cm of seam unstitched at the top of the seam. Pin top of sleeve into top of armhole, and pin the unstitched section of the sleeve seam across the straight cast-off edge at the base of the armhole. Sew in place and repeat for other sleeve. Press seams lightly from wrong side.

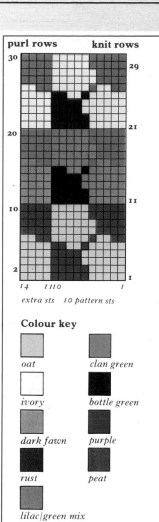

purl rows   **knit rows**

14 11 10   1

extra sts   *10 pattern sts*

Colour key

oat   clan green

ivory   bottle green

dark fawn   purple

rust   peat

lilac/green mix

SQUARES ON BLACK

A striking geometric design of small boxes of colour
bounded with black makes this peplum jacket a smart and unusual garment.
The pattern incorporates bands of black garter stitch.

purl rows   knit rows

50 / 49
42 / 43
garter st
36 / 37
29
28
garter st
22 / 23
15
14
garter st
8 / 9
2 / 1

8 pattern sts

Colour key

- black
- yellow
- peat
- sage green
- pink
- rust
- ivory
- green
- lilac/green mix
- bluebell

MATERIALS

Yarn
Use 2-ply jumper weight Shetland yarn.
Yarn A 150g *(black)*
Yarn B 50g *(yellow)*
Yarn C 50g *(peat)*
Yarn D 50g *(sage green)*
Yarn E 50g *(pink)*
Yarn F 50g *(rust)*
Yarn G 50g *(ivory)*
Yarn H 50g *(green)*
Yarn J 50g *(lilac/green mix)*
Yarn K 50g *(bluebell)*

Needles
1 pair size 3¼mm
1 pair size 2¾mm
1 crochet hook size 2¾mm

Notions
1 button

MEASUREMENTS

To fit bust 86 (91, 97)cm (34, 36, 38in).
(See also chart on p. 117.)

Tension
32 sts and 34 rows measure 10cm over
Fair Isle pattern on 3¼mm needles.

BACK

Peplum skirt
With 2¾mm needles and yarn A, cast on
272 (288, 304) sts. Work 6 rows in st st in
yarn A. Then knit 2 rows to form hemline. Change to 3¼mm needles and work
8 rows in st st in yarn A, starting with a
knit row.
Now work Fair Isle pattern from chart,
reading odd (knit) rows from right to left
and even (purl) rows from left to right,
except for rows 9–16, 23–30, 37–44
inclusive which are all knit rows forming
wide bands of garter stitch. Repeat the 8
pattern sts 34 (36, 38) times across the
rows. Continue in pattern until you have
worked row 2 (8, 8) of the second working
of the pattern chart and the work measures
approx. 17 (19, 19)cm from hemline.
Decrease for waist across next row as
follows: (yarn A), k2 tog right across row –
136 (144, 152) sts. Change to 2¾mm needles
and work 9 rows in k1, p1 twisted rib.
Change to 3¼mm needles and st st and
continue pattern from row 3 (15, 15) of the
second working of the pattern chart,
until you have completed row 14 (28, 32)
of the third working of the pattern chart
and back measures approximately 18 (19,
20)cm from top of waistband.
Shape armholes: Continuing in pattern,
cast off 8 sts at the beginning of the next
2 rows. Then k2 tog at each end of the
next 9 rows – 102 (110, 118) sts. Now
work straight in pattern until you have
completed row 32 of the fourth working of
chart (row 50 of fourth working, row 8 of
fifth working) and armhole measures
approximately 19 (20, 22)cm from start of
armhole shaping.
Shape shoulders: Continuing in pattern,
cast off 8 sts at the beginning of the next
4 rows; then cast off 5 (6, 7) sts at the
beginning of the next 6 rows. Transfer the
remaining 40 (42, 44) sts to a spare needle
or stitch holder.

FRONTS

Left front
With 2¾mm needles and yarn A, cast on
120 (128, 136) sts. Work 6 rows in st st in
yarn A. Then knit 2 rows to form hemline.
Change to 3¼mm needles and work 8
more rows in st st in yarn A, starting with
a knit row.
Now work Fair Isle pattern from chart,
repeating the 8 pattern sts 15 (16, 17)
times across the rows. Continue in pattern
until you have completed row 2 (8, 8) of
the second working of the pattern chart
and work measures approximately 17 (19,
19)cm from hemline. Then decrease for
waist as follows: *for the smaller size,*
(k2 tog, k3 tog) four times, (k2 tog) forty
times, (k3 tog, k2 tog) four times; *for the
medium size,* k2 tog right across row; *for*

the larger size, k4, (k2 tog) sixty-four
times, k4 – 56 (64, 72) sts.
Waistband: Change to 2¾mm needles
and work 9 rows in k1, p1 twisted rib in
yarn A.
Change to 3¼mm needles and st st and
work Fair Isle pattern from chart, beginning at row 3 (15, 15) of the second
working of the pattern chart. Continue in
pattern until you have completed row 14
(28, 32) of the third working of the pattern
chart and the front measures approximately 18 (19, 20)cm from the top of the
waistband.
Shape armhole: Continuing in pattern,
cast off 4 (6, 7) sts at the beginning of the
next row. Then work one row straight.
K2 tog at the armhole edge on the next 7
(9, 10) rows – 45 (49, 55) sts. Now continue in pattern without further shaping
until you have completed row 11 (29, 33)
of the fourth working of the pattern chart.
Shape neck: With wrong side facing,
cast off 3 (3, 4) sts at the beginning of the
next row. Then k2 tog at the neck edge on
every row until 31 (34, 37) sts remain.
Work straight in pattern until you have
worked row 32 of the fourth working of
the chart (row 50 of the fourth working of
the chart, row 8 of the fifth working of the
chart), and armhole measures approximately 19 (20, 22)cm from the start of the
armhole shaping.
Shape shoulder: Cast off 8 sts at the
beginning of next and following alternate
row; cast off 5 (6, 7) sts at the beginning
of the following 3 alternate rows.

Right front
Work in the same way as left front,
matching pattern, but reversing shapings.

SLEEVES

With 2¾mm needles and yarn A, cast on
62 (62, 64) sts and work 6cm in k1, p1
twisted rib, increasing across the last
(wrong-side) row as follows: rib 10 (10, 8)
sts, *make one st, rib one st; repeat from *
to last 11 (11, 9) sts; make one st, rib to
end of row – 104 (104, 112) sts.
Change to 3¼mm needles and, starting at
row 37 (43, 43) of chart, work straight in
pattern until you have worked row 14 (28,
32) of the third working of the chart and
the sleeve measures approximately 41 (43,
44)cm from cast-on edge.
Shape top of sleeve: Continuing in
pattern, cast off 8 sts at the beginning of
the next 2 rows. Then k2 tog at each end
of the next and every following alternate
row, 7 (10, 12) times. Work 13 (15, 15)
rows straight in pattern. K2 tog at each
end of the next and following alternate
row, 11 (8, 8) times. Purl one row. Cast
off remaining sts fairly tightly. Make
another sleeve in the same way.

FRONT BANDS

Begin by joining fronts to back at shoulders.

Left front

With 2¾mm needles and yarn A, pick up and knit 189 (189, 197) sts down front opening edge as far as hemline. Work 9 rows in k1, p1 twisted rib in yarn A, increasing one st at the neck edge on rows 4 and 8. Cast off in rib.

Right front

Beginning at hemline, with right side facing, pick up and knit 189 (189, 197) sts up front opening edge to start of neck shaping. Work to correspond with left front band.

NECKBAND

With right side facing, using 2¾mm needles and yarn A, starting at beginning of neck shaping on right front and leaving front bands free, pick up and knit 117 (119, 121) sts around the neck as far as the start of neck shaping on left front, including the sts on the stitch holder at the back of the neck. Work 8 (10, 10) rows in st st in yarn A, starting with a purl row. Then knit 2 rows to form foldline of neckband. Work a further 8 (10, 10) rows in st st. Cast off.

TO MAKE UP

Press all pieces lightly from wrong side avoiding ribbing. Join side and sleeve seams. Sew in sleeves, easing fullness at top of sleeves to fit armholes. Turn under the 6 rows of st st around hem to inside, following garter stitch hemline, and slip stitch inner cast-on edge in position on inside. Oversew edges of hem at each side of front opening to jacket fronts. Turn in the 8 (10) rows of st st around neckband to inside, following garter stitch foldline, and slip stitch inner cast-off edge in position around neck. Oversew the two edges of neckband together on either side of front opening. Crochet a chain loop for button (see p. 141) and sew in position at right front waistband. Sew a button to left band to match. Press all seams from wrong side.

COPPER DIAMONDS

A loose fitting crew neck sweater. The subtle blue and beige stripes are brought out with specks of copper yarn, but these could be replaced with Shetland yarn for a softer effect.

MATERIALS

Yarn

Use 2-ply jumper weight Shetland yarn unless otherwise indicated. Different sizes will require different quantities of yarn.
Yarn A 100 (100, 100, 125)g *(blue/orange mix)*
Yarn B 50 (50, 50, 75)g *(blue/fawn mix)*
Yarn C 50g *(mid-blue mix)*
Yarn D 50 (50, 50, 75)g lurex *(copper)*
Yarn E 50 (50, 50, 75)g *(mid-brown mix)*

Yarn F 25 (25, 25, 50)g *(oat)*
Yarn G 25g *(bright blue)*
Yarn H 25 (25, 25, 50)g *(rust/blue mix)*
Yarn J 25g *(tan)*

Needles

1 pair size 3¼mm
1 pair size 2¾mm

MEASUREMENTS

To fit chest 84 (91, 99, 107)cm (33, 36, 39, 42in).
(See also chart on p. 117.)

Tension

30 sts and 32 rows measure 10cm over Fair Isle pattern on 3¼mm needles.

BACK

**With 2¾mm needles and yarn A, cast on 118 (130, 142, 152) sts. Work 4 (5, 5, 6)cm in k1, p1 twisted rib in yarn A, increasing across the last wrong-side row as follows: rib 6 (4, 2, 8) sts, *rib twice into the next st, rib 7 (8, 9, 8) sts; repeat from * 13 (13, 13, 15) more times – 132 (144, 156, 168) sts. Change to 3¼mm needles and st st and work Fair Isle pattern from chart, reading odd (knit) rows from right to left and even (purl) rows from left to right. Repeat the 12 pattern sts indicated on chart 11 (12, 13, 14) times across each row. Continuing in pattern, work straight until you have worked row 52 (56, 64, 64) of the second working of the pattern chart and the back measures approximately 41 (43, 45, 46)cm from the cast-on edge.

Shape armholes: Cast off 8 (12, 12, 16) sts at the beginning of the next 2 rows – 116 (120, 132, 136) sts remain**. Then work armhole edges straight, continuing in pattern until you have worked row 50 (54, 66, 4) of the third (third, third, fourth) working of the pattern chart, and the back measures approximately 60 (63, 66, 69)cm from cast-on edge.

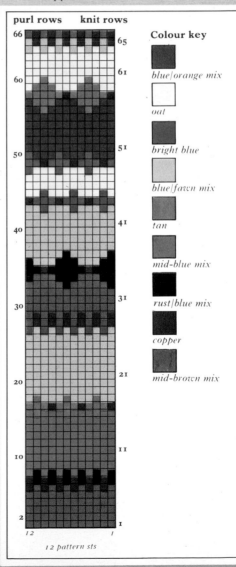

Shape shoulders:
Cast off 12 (13, 15, 15) sts at the beginning of the next 2 rows. Cast off 12 (12, 13, 14) sts at the beginning of the following 4 rows. Leave remaining 44 (46, 50, 50) sts on a spare needle.

FRONT

Work as for back from ** to ** – 116 (120, 132, 136) sts. Continuing in pattern, work straight until you have completed row 34 (40, 46, 52) of the third working of chart, and front measures approximately 51 (53, 56, 58)cm from cast-on edge.

Shape neck: On the next (right-side) row, work the pattern across the first 42 (44, 48, 50) sts in the row, cast off the next 32 (32, 36, 36) sts and then work the pattern across the remaining 42 (44, 48, 50) sts in the row. Now shape neck edge on these last 42 (44, 48, 50) sts by decreasing one st at the (inner) neck edge on the next 6 (7, 7, 7) rows – 36 (37, 41, 43) sts remain. Then work straight until you have completed row 52 (56, 64, 64) of the second working of the pattern chart and front measures the same as the back from cast-on edge – approximately 60 (63, 66, 69)cm.

Shape shoulder: Cast off 12 (13, 15, 15) sts at the beginning of the next row. Then cast off 12 (12, 13, 14) sts at the beginning of the following 4 rows. With wrong side of work facing, rejoin the yarn to the remaining 42 (44, 48, 50) sts of the left side of neck. Work left neck edge and shoulder to correspond with right neck edge and shoulder, reversing shapings.

SLEEVES

With 2¾mm needles and yarn A, cast on 58 (58, 60, 60) sts. Work 8 (9, 9, 9)cm in k1, p1 twisted rib in yarn A. Change to 3¼mm needles and st st and work Fair Isle pattern from chart, beginning at row 1 as before, *at the same time* shaping the sides by increasing one st at each end of the 3rd and every following 4th row, until there are 128 (128, 136, 144) sts on the needle. Take the extra sts into the pattern as they are made. When there are 128 (128, 136, 144) sts on the needle, work straight until the sleeve measures approximately 51 (52, 53, 54)cm from cast-on edge. Cast off right across row (this cast-off edge must measure approximately 41 (41, 43, 45)cm across to fit armhole.
Make another sleeve in the same way.

NECKBAND

Join right shoulder seam.
With right side of work facing, using 2¾mm needles and yarn A, beginning at the left shoulder, pick up and knit 36 (36, 38, 38) sts down left side of neck, 32 (32, 34, 34) sts across centre-front, 36 (36, 38, 38) sts up right side of neck and the 44 (46, 50, 50) sts on spare needle at back of neck – 148 (150, 160, 160) sts in all. Work 13 rows in k1, p1 twisted rib in yarn A. Cast off in rib in yarn A.

TO MAKE UP

Press all pieces from the wrong side, avoiding ribbing. Join left shoulder seam and side seams. Join underarm sleeve seam, leaving 2 (4, 4, 5)cm unstitched at the top of seam. Pin sleeve into armhole, pinning unstitched section of sleeve seam across straight cast-off edge at bottom of armhole. Sew in place. Repeat for other sleeve. Press seams from wrong side.

purl rows   knit rows

Colour key

- blue/orange mix
- oat
- bright blue
- blue/fawn mix
- tan
- mid-blue mix
- rust/blue mix
- copper
- mid-brown mix

12 pattern sts

MAURICE

Men's or women's Fair Isle waistcoat with striped rib back.
The shawl collar is worked separately and sewn over
the top of the front bands.

MATERIALS

Yarn
Use 2-ply jumper weight Shetland yarn.
Different sizes require different quantities
of main yarn.
Yarn A 100 (100, 125)g *(blue/wine mix)*
Yarn B 50g *(peat)*
Yarn C 50g *(lilac/green mix)*
Yarn D 50g *(pale green mix)*
Yarn E 50g *(rust mix)*
Yarn F 25g *(rust/blue mix)*
Yarn G 25g *(pale lilac mix)*
Yarn H 25g *(rust)*
Yarn J 25g *(dark fawn)*
Yarn K 25g *(pale pink mix)*

Needles
1 pair size 3¼mm
1 pair size 3mm
1 pair size 2¾mm

Notions
5 buttons

MEASUREMENTS

To fit chest 91 (97, 102)cm (36, 38, 40in).
(See also chart on p. 117.)

Tension
32 sts and 32 rows measure 10cm over
Fair Isle pattern on 3¼mm needles.

back of waistcoat

FRONTS

Pocket linings
Begin by making the pocket linings as
follows; with 3mm needles and yarn A,
cast on 28 (30, 32) sts. Work 6cm in st st
ending with a purl row. Leave sts on a
spare needle and repeat for other pocket.

Left front
With 2¾mm needles and yarn A, cast on
68 (72, 80) sts. Work 5cm in k1, p1 twisted
rib in yarn A, increasing across the last
(wrong-side) row as follows: *purl 16 (11,
19) sts, purl twice into the next st; repeat
from * 3 (5, 3) more times – 72 (78,
84) sts.
Change to 3¼mm needles and st st and
work Fair Isle pattern from chart, reading
odd (knit) rows from right to left and even
(purl) rows from left to right. Work the
pattern across knit rows as follows: *for the
small size* (91cm), repeat sts *1–12* six
times; *for the medium size* (97cm), repeat
sts *1–12* six times and then work sts *1–6*
once to complete row; *for the large size*
(102cm), work sts *1–12* seven times. Work
purl rows in reverse. Continue thus in
pattern until you have completed row 18
(20, 20) of the pattern chart.

Pocket: Introduce pocket in row 19 (21,
21) as follows: work the first 22 (24, 26)
sts in row, slip the next 28 (30, 32) sts on
to a spare needle and in their place work
the pattern across the 28 (30, 32) sts of
one pocket lining on spare needle; work
the pattern to the end of the row.
Continue straight in pattern until you
have completed row 76 (4, 8) of the first
(second, second) working of the pattern
chart and front measures approximately
29 (30, 32)cm from cast-on edge.

Shape armhole and neck edge: Cast
off 14 (15, 16) sts at the beginning of the
next row, then work pattern to last 2 sts,
k2 tog. Continuing in pattern, decrease
one st at the armhole edge on the next 15
(15, 17) rows – 29 (30, 33) sts should have
been decreased in all – then work armhole
edge straight. *At the same time,* decrease
one st at the neck edge on every following
5th (4th, 4th) row after the first decrease
on row 1 (5, 9), until you have decreased
13 (16, 18) sts at neck edge – 30 (32, 33)
sts remain. Now work straight until you
have worked row 72 (4, 16) of the second
(third, third) working of the pattern chart
and the front measures approximately 51
(55, 57)cm from cast-on edge.

Shape shoulder: Continuing in pattern, cast off 10 (12, 11) sts at the beginning of the next row. Then cast off 10 (10, 11) sts at the beginning of the following 2 alternate rows.

Right front
Work as for left front, reversing pocket, armhole, neck and shoulder shapings.

BACK

With 2¾mm needles and yarn A, cast on 144 (156, 168) sts. Work 5cm in k1, p1 twisted rib, ending on a wrong-side row. Change to 3mm needles and continue to work entire back in twisted rib in the following five-colour stripe sequence:
Row 1: Yarn A
Row 2: Yarn D
Row 3: Yarn H
Row 4: Yarn J
Row 5: Yarn E

Continue repeating rows 1–5 up the back, carrying yarns not in use up the sides of the work, until back measures approximately 29 (30, 32)cm from cast-on edge, ending with a wrong-side row.
Shape armholes: Continuing in rib, cast off 4 (5, 6) sts at the beginning of the next 2 rows. Then k2 tog at each end of the next 16 (17, 18) rows – 104 (112, 120) sts remain. Then work straight in striped rib until back measures the same as the front from cast-on edge to start of shoulder shaping – approximately 51 (55, 57)cm – ending on a wrong-side row.
Shape shoulders: Continuing in striped rib, cast off 10 (12, 11) sts at the beginning of the next 2 rows. Then cast off 10 (10, 11) sts at the beginning of the following 4 rows; divide the remaining 44 (48, 54) sts in half and transfer each half to a spare

needle or stitch holder.

Join fronts to back at shoulders.

FRONT BANDS

Right front
With 2¾mm needles and yarn A, with right side facing and beginning at lower edge, pick up and knit 93 (97, 101) sts up front opening edge to start of neck shaping; then pick up and knit a further 89 (93, 101) sts around the side of the neck including the 22 (24, 27) sts on first spare needle at back of neck. Work 3 rows in k1, p1 twisted rib in yarn A.
Buttonholes: Make 5 buttonholes in the 4th row of ribbing as follows: rib 4 sts, *cast off 3 sts, rib 18 (19, 20) sts; repeat from * three more times, cast off 3 sts, rib to end of row. Rib back along the next row casting on 3 sts directly over those cast off in the previous row. Work 4 more rows in rib in yarn A. Join in yarn B and work a further row in rib in yarn B. Cast off in rib in yarn B.

Left front
With right side facing, using 2¾mm needles and yarn D, beginning at the centre-back of the neck rib the 22 (24, 27) sts from the remaining spare needle at the back of the neck and then pick up and knit a further 67 (69, 74) sts down to start of neck shaping and then 93 (97, 101) sts down front opening edge. Work to correspond with right front band, omitting buttonholes.

ARMHOLE BANDS

With right side facing, using 2¾mm needles and yarn A, pick up and knit 142 (150, 166) sts around one armhole. Work 9 rows of twisted rib in yarn A. Join in yarn B and work a further row in rib in yarn B. Cast off in rib in yarn B.
Repeat for other armhole.

POCKET TOPS

With right side facing, using 2¾mm needles and yarn A, knit across the 28 (30, 32) sts for one pocket on spare needle. Work 7 rows in twisted rib in yarn A. Join in yarn B and work a further row of rib in yarn B. Cast off in rib in yarn B.
Repeat for other pocket top.

SHAWL COLLAR

With 3mm needles and yarn A, cast on 191 (195, 201) sts. Work 9 rows in k1, p1 twisted rib. Continue in rib and shape collar by casting off 2 sts at the beginning of the next 24 rows. Then cast off 6 sts at the beginning of the following 16 rows – 47 (51, 57) sts remain. Cast off in rib.

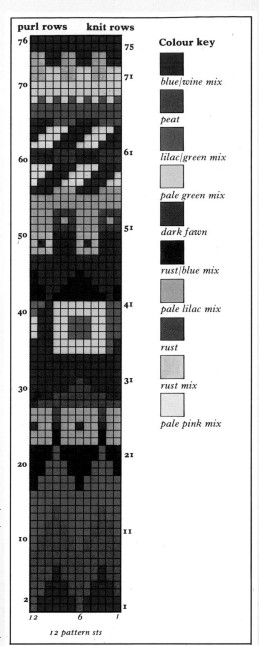

TO MAKE UP

Press pieces lightly from the wrong side, avoiding ribbing. Join fronts to back at side seams. Join front bands together at centre-back. Sew the three free sides of each pocket lining to the back of the waistcoat fronts. Sew down the sides of each pocket top. Pin centre of shaped collar piece to the centre back of neck, inside the ribbed front band and then pin the rest of the edge of the collar around the neck edge to start of neck shaping on each side. Stitch collar in position and then fold it over so that it covers the ribbed border. Catch down at front edges to hold in position. Press collar lightly to hold fold. Sew on five buttons to left front band to match buttonholes. Press seams lightly from wrong side.

FLOWERS

WALLFLOWERS

*This boat neck cotton sweater with repeating Wallflower motifs
is interspersed with bands of écru Turkish stitch. The wide ribbing
at the sleeve and neck is bordered with a contrasting yarn.*

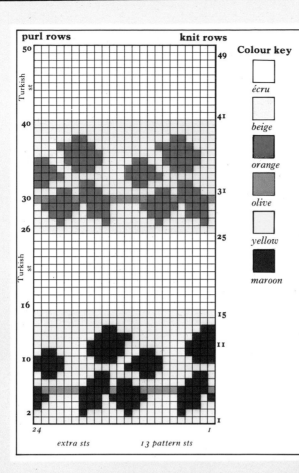

purl rows   **knit rows**

Colour key

☐ écru

☐ beige

■ orange

▦ olive

☐ yellow

■ maroon

extra sts   13 pattern sts

as follows: (row 16) k1, *yfwd, sl 1, k1, pass slipped st over; repeat from * to last st; k1. Work 9 more rows in the same way (see also p. 130 for Turkish stitch). Now work the next 15 rows of Wallflower pattern from chart as before starting at row 26. Then work rows 41–50 in Turkish stitch to complete one working of pattern chart. Work rows 1–40 inclusive again. The work should now measure approximately 35 (37)cm from cast-on edge.

Shape armholes: Continuing in pattern (row 41, Turkish stitch) cast off 10 (12) sts at the beginning of the next 2 rows – 124 (130) sts. Then work straight until you have completed row 25 of the third working of the pattern chart.

Change to 2¼mm needles and yarn A and work 11cm in k1, p1 twisted rib, to form ribbing for boat neck. Change to yarn E and work a further row in twisted rib in yarn E. Cast off in rib in yarn E.

Make another piece in the same way.

SLEEVES

With 2¼mm needles and yarn E, cast on 60 sts. Work one row of k1, p1 twisted rib in yarn E. Change to yarn A and continue in twisted rib for 10cm, increasing across the last (wrong-side) row as follows: *rib 2, rib twice into next st; repeat from * 19 more times – 80 sts.

Change to 3¼mm needles and work pattern from chart, repeating the basic 13 pattern sts (1–13) six times across the row and working the extra 2 sts (14–15) at the end of knit rows and at the beginning of purl rows. *At the same time,* shape sides by increasing one st at each end of the 3rd and every following 4th row until there are 134 sts on the needle, taking the extra sts into the pattern as they are made. Then work straight in pattern until you have completed row 25 of the third working of the pattern chart, and the sleeve measures approximately 49cm from cast-on edge. Cast off right across row.

Make another sleeve in the same way.

TO MAKE UP

Press all pieces lightly from wrong side avoiding ribbing. Join front to back at side seams. Join each sleeve seam leaving 4cm at top of seam unstitched. Overlap 4cm of front neck ribbing over back neck ribbing and hold each side with a pin. Sew the ribbings together from shoulder edge to point 4cm in from shoulder edge on each side, sewing just underneath the edge of the front ribbing so that stitches are invisible. Pin sleeves into armholes, pinning each side of unstitched section of sleeve seam across straight cast-off edge at bottom of armholes. Sew sleeves in position. Press seams from wrong side.

MATERIALS

Yarn
Use No. 8 cotton yarn.
Yarn A 350g *(écru)*
Yarn B 250g *(beige)*
Yarn C 100g *(orange)*
Yarn D 100g *(maroon)*
Yarn E 50g *(olive)*
Yarn F 50g *(yellow)*

Needles
1 pair size 3¼mm
1 pair size 2¼mm

BACK and FRONT

Work the front and back in the same way. With 2¼mm needles and yarn A, cast on 128 (136) sts. Work 7 (9)cm in k1, p1 twisted rib in yarn A increasing across the last (wrong-side) row as follows: *rib 4 (3) sts, rib twice into the next st, rib 3 sts; repeat from * 15 (17) more times – 144 (154) sts.

Change to 3¼mm needles and st st and work Wallflower pattern from chart, reading odd (knit) rows from right to left and even (purl) rows from left to right. Work the pattern across knit rows as follows: repeat the basic 13 pattern sts indicated on chart (1–13) eleven times across row *for both sizes,* and then work st *14 for the smaller size,* and sts *14–24 for the larger size,* to finish row. Work purl rows in reverse starting with the extra sts. Work rows 1–15 of the chart. Then work the next 10 rows (16–25) in Turkish stitch

MEASUREMENTS

To fit chest 91 (97)cm (36, 38in). *(See also chart on p. 118.)*

Tension
31 sts and 32 rows measure 10cm over Wallflowers pattern on 3¼mm needles.

IRIS

*A pretty feminine cardigan of yellow and purple Irises,
bordered with mohair. The cardigan has a moss stitch collar
and front pockets.*

MATERIALS

Yarn
Use 2-ply jumper weight Shetland yarn
unless otherwise indicated.
Yarn A 100g *(pale lilac mix)*
Yarn B 75g *(lilac/green mix)*
Yarn C 25g *(violet)*
Yarn D 25g *(purple)*
Yarn E 25g *(sage green)*
Yarn F 25g *(wine)*
Yarn G 25g *(pale yellow)*
Yarn H 25g *(yellow)*
Yarn K 25g lurex *(gold)*
Yarn L 100g mohair *(wine mix)*

Needles
1 pair size 3¼mm
1 pair size 3mm
1 pair size 2¾mm
1 pair size 2¼mm

Notions
7 buttons

MEASUREMENTS

To fit bust 86 (91)cm (34, 36in).
(See also chart on p. 118.)

Tension

30 sts and 36 rows measure 10cm over
Fair Isle pattern on 3¼mm needles.

BACK

With 2¾mm needles and yarn B, cast on
124 (130) sts. Work 5 (6)cm in k1, p1
twisted rib in yarn B, increasing across the
last (wrong-side) row as follows: rib 2 sts,
*rib twice into the next st, rib 9 (8) sts;
repeat from * 11 (13) more times, rib 2 sts
– 136 (144) sts.
Change to 3¼mm needles and st st and
work pattern from chart, reading odd
(knit) rows from right to left and even
(purl) rows from left to right. Work the
pattern across knit rows as follows: *for the
smaller size (86cm)*, repeat sts 1–16, eight
times across the row and then work sts
1–8 once to complete the row; *for the
larger size (91cm)*, repeat sts 1–16, nine

times across the row. Work purl rows in
reverse. Continuing in pattern, work
straight until you have completed row 22
of the chart. Now work rows 23–28
inclusive in reversed st st in mohair as
follows: row 23, knit; row 24, knit; row
25, purl; row 26, knit; row 28, purl.
Then continue in pattern from row 29
to the end of row 50. Work rows 51–56
in reversed st st in the same way as rows
23–28. Repeat chart until you have
worked row 36 (second working) and back
measures approximately 30 (31)cm from
the cast-on edge.
Shape armholes: Continuing in pattern,
cast off 6 (8) sts at the beginning of the
next 2 rows. Then decrease one st at each

end of every row
until 100 (108) sts remain.
Work straight in pattern until
you have worked row 50 (54) of the
third working of chart and back measures
approximately 51 (52)cm from cast-on edge.
Shape shoulders: Cast off 6 sts at the
beginning of the next 4 rows. Then cast
off 6 (7) sts at the beginning of the next 6
rows; cast off remaining 40 (42) sts.

FRONTS

Pocket linings
Begin by making pocket linings. With
3mm needles and yarn B, cast on 28 (30)
sts. Work 6cm in st st, ending with a knit
row. Leave the sts on a spare needle and
work another lining in the same way.

Left front
With 2¾mm needles and yarn B, cast on
54 (58) sts. Work 5 (6)cm in k1, p1 twisted
rib, increasing across last (wrong-side) row
as follows: rib 3 (1) sts, *rib 5 (6) sts, rib
twice into next st; repeat from * 7 more
times, rib 3 (1) sts – 62 (66) sts.

Change to 3¼mm needles and st st and work pattern from chart. Work the pattern across knit rows as follows: *for the smaller size*, repeat sts 1–16, three times, then work sts 1–14 once to complete the row; *for the larger size*, repeat sts 1–16 four times then work sts 1–2 once to complete the row. Work purl rows in reverse. Continue thus in pattern until you have worked row 20 of the chart.

Pocket: Introduce pocket in row 21 as follows: work the first 17 (18) sts in the row, cast off the next 28 (30) sts, then continue the pattern to end of row. On the next row (row 22), work the pattern across the first 17 (18) sts of row and then

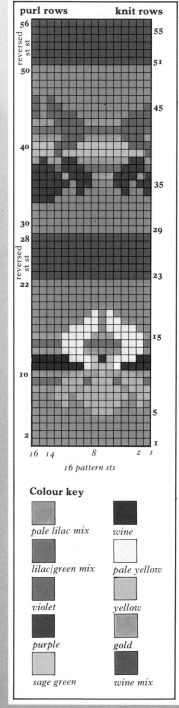

purl rows   knit rows

56
reversed
st st   55

50   51

45

40

35

30   29
28
reversed
st st   23

22

15

10
5

2   1

16 14   8   2 1

16 pattern sts

Colour key

pale lilac mix   wine

lilac/green mix   pale yellow

violet   yellow

purple   gold

sage green   wine mix

continue in pattern across the 28 (30) sts of one pocket lining on spare needle; then work pattern to end of row. Continue in pattern from row 23 of chart until you have worked row 36 of the second working of the chart and the front measures approximately 30 (31)cm from cast-on edge.
Shape armholes: Continuing in pattern, cast off 8 (10) sts at the beginning of the next row. Then k2 tog at armhole edge on the next 10 (8) rows – 44 (48) sts remain. Now work straight until you have completed row 29 (33) of the third working of the chart and front measures approximately 43 (47)cm from cast-on edge.
Shape neck: Continuing in pattern, cast off 3 sts at the beginning of the next row; then k2 tog at the neck edge on the next 11 (12) rows – 30 (33) sts remain. Work straight in pattern, until you have worked row 50 (54) of the third working of the chart and the front measures approximately 51 (52)cm from cast-on edge.
Shape shoulder: Cast off 6 sts at the beginning of the next and following alternate row. Cast off 6 (7) sts at the beginning of the following 3 alternate rows.

Right front
Work in the same way as left front, but reverse pocket, armhole, neck and shoulder shapings.

SLEEVES

With 2¾mm needles and yarn B, cast on 62 sts. Work 5 (6)cm in k1, p1 twisted rib, increasing across the last wrong-side row as follows: rib 10 sts, rib twice into the next 42 sts, rib 10 sts – 104 sts.
Change to 3¼mm needles and st st and work pattern from chart, beginning on row 23 of the chart. Work rows 23 to 29 inclusive in reversed st st as before. Then work the pattern across knit rows as

follows: repeat sts 1–16 six times across the row and then work sts 1–8 once to complete the row. Work purl rows in reverse. Continue in pattern until you have worked row 36 of the third working of the chart and sleeve measures approximately 41 (42)cm from cast-on edge.

Shape top of sleeve: Continuing in pattern, cast off 8 sts at the beginning of the next 2 rows; then k2 tog at each end of the next and every following alternate row, ten times – 68 sts. Now work 17 (19) rows straight. Then k2 tog at each end of the next and every following alternate row five times. K2 tog at each end of the following 7 rows – 44 sts remain. Cast off. Make another sleeve in the same way.

FRONT BANDS

Right front
With 2¾mm needles and yarn B, with right side of work facing and beginning at lower edge, pick up and knit 159 (165) sts up front opening edge to start of neck shaping. Work 5 rows in k1, p1 twisted rib.
Buttonholes: Make 7 buttonholes in the 6th row of ribbing as follows: rib 4 sts, *cast off 3 sts, rib 22 (23) sts; repeat from * five more times, cast off 3 sts, rib 2 sts. Rib back across next row, casting on 3 sts over those cast off in previous row. Work 4 more rows in rib, then cast off.

Left front
Beginning at start of neck shaping pick up and knit 159 (165) sts down the front opening edge. Work to correspond with right front band but omit buttonholes.

COLLAR

With 2¼mm needles and yarn B, cast on 39 (43) sts and work the collar in moss stitch (i.e. work every row k1, p1 to last st, k1. Cast on 5 sts at the beginning of the next 10 rows after the first row. Then cast on 7 (8) sts at the beginning of the following 2 rows – 103 (109) sts. Work a further 6cm in moss st. Cast off in moss st.

POCKET TOPS

With right side facing, 2¾mm needles and yarn B, pick up and knit 28 (30) sts across cast-off edge of one pocket. Work 10 rows in k1, p1 twisted rib; cast off. Work other pocket top in same way.

TO MAKE UP

Press all pieces lightly from wrong side, avoiding ribbing. Join shoulder and side and sleeve seams. Pin and sew sleeves into armholes, gathering top of sleeves to fit. Pin shaped edge of collar around neck between inner edges of front bands. Sew in position with a flat seam sewn from the under side. Sew down sides of pocket tops and linings. Sew on buttons.

MARIGOLD

Yellow Marigolds interspersed with bands of mohair
worked in reverse stocking stitch. The waistcoat has front pockets
and the back is worked in striped rib.

MATERIALS

Yarn

Use 2-ply jumper weight Shetland yarn
unless otherwise indicated. Different sizes
require different quantities of main yarn.

Yarn A 100 (100, 125)g *(brown-green mix)*

Yarn B 50g *(rust)*

Yarn C 25g *(yellow)*

Yarn D 25g *(dark orange mix)*

Yarn E 50g lurex *(copper)*

Yarn F 50g *(chocolate)*

Yarn G 25g *(clan green)*

Yarn H 50g mohair *(brown mix)*

Needles

1 pair size 3¼mm

1 pair size 3mm

1 pair size 2¾mm

Notions

5 buttons

MEASUREMENTS

To fit chest 84 (91, 99)cm (33, 36, 39in).
(See also chart on p. 118.)

Tension

32 sts and 30 rows measure 10cm over
Fair Isle pattern on 3¼mm needles.

FRONTS

Pocket linings

With 2¾mm needles and yarn A, cast on
28 (32, 36) sts. Work 7cm in st st in yarn
A, ending with a purl row. Leave sts on a
spare needle or stitch holder. Repeat for
other pocket lining.

Left front

**With 2¾mm needles and yarn A, cast on
60 (66, 72) sts. Work 5cm in k1, p1 twisted
rib, increasing 6 sts evenly across the last

back of waistcoat

(wrong-side) row, by working twice into every 10th (11th, 12th) st, 6 times – 66 (72, 78) sts**.
Change to 3¼mm needles and st st and work Fair Isle pattern from chart, reading odd (knit) rows from right to left and even (purl) rows from left to right. Work the pattern across the knit rows as follows: repeat the basic 16 pattern sts (*1–16*) four times across row *for all sizes,* and then work sts *1–2 (1–8, 1–14)* once to finish the row. Work purl rows in reverse, working the extra sts at the beginning of the row. Continue in pattern until you have worked row 20 of the pattern chart.
Pocket: Introduce pocket in row 21 as follows: knit the first 19 (20, 21) sts of row in pattern, then slip the next 28 (32, 36) sts on to a spare needle or stitch holder and in their place continue to work the

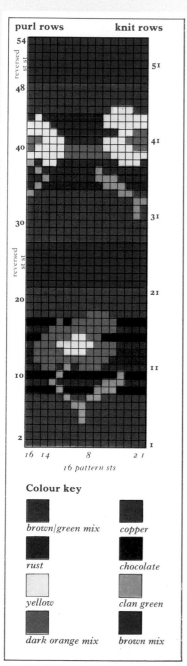

purl rows   **knit rows**

54
reversed st st
51
48

41
40

31
30

reversed st st
21
20

11
10

2
1

16 14   8   2 1
16 pattern sts

Colour key

brown/green mix   copper

rust   chocolate

yellow   clan green

dark orange mix   brown mix

pattern across the 28 (32, 36) sts of one pocket lining piece on spare needle; continue in pattern to end of row. Work rows 22–27 of chart in reversed st st in mohair as follows: row 22, knit; row 23, knit; row 24, purl; row 25, knit; row 26, purl; row 27, knit. Continue to work rows 28–48 in pattern from chart, then work rows 49–54 in reversed st st in mohair as follows: row 49, purl; row 50, purl; row 51, knit; row 52, purl; row 53, knit; row 54, purl. The 54 rows of one complete pattern chart have now been worked.
Continue in pattern until you have completed row 14 (18, 20) of the second working of pattern and front measures approx. 28 (29, 30)cm from cast-on edge.
Shape armhole and neck: At the beginning of the next row, cast off 8 (10, 12) sts and then work pattern across to the last 2 sts; k2 tog. Continuing in pattern, decrease one st at the armhole edge on the next 12 (14, 16) rows. Then work armhole edge straight. *At the same time,* decrease one st at the neck edge on every following 4th row after the first decrease, 8 (9, 13) times in all. Then decrease one st at neck edge on every following 3rd row until 26 (28, 30) sts remain. Then work neck edge straight in pattern until you have completed row 28 of the third working of pattern chart. Work a few rows straight in st st and yarn A only (to avoid having broken pattern) until front measures approx. 52 (54, 57)cm from cast-on edge.
Shape shoulder: Cast off 10 sts at the beginning of the next right-side row. Then cast off 8 (9, 10) sts at the beginning of the following 2 alternate rows.

Right front
Work in same way as for left front from ** to **. Change to 3¼mm needles and work pattern from chart, repeating the basic 16 pattern sts four times across the rows and the extra 2 (8, 14) sts at the end of knit rows and at the beginning of purl rows as before. Work to correspond with left front, taking in remaining pocket lining and reversing neck, armhole and shoulder shapings.

BACK

With 2¾mm needles and yarn A, cast on 128 (140, 152) sts. Work 5cm in k1, p1 twisted rib in yarn A, increasing across the last (wrong-side) row by working twice into every 32nd (35th, 38th) st, four times – 132 (144, 156) sts.
Change to 3mm needles and work entire back in twisted rib, in the following three-colour stripe sequence:
Row 1: Yarn A
Row 2: Yarn B
Row 3: Yarn C
Continue working back straight, repeating rows 1–3 until back measures approximately 28 (29, 30)cm from cast-on edge, ending on a wrong-side row.
Shape armholes: Cast off 3 (4, 6) sts at the beginning of the next 2 rows; then k2 tog at each end of every row until 100

(108, 116) sts remain. Then work straight until back measures the same as the fronts from the start of the armhole shaping to the start of the shoulder shaping – approximately 52 (54, 57)cm.
Shape shoulders: On next right-side row, cast off 10 (10, 11) sts at beginning of this and next row. Cast off 9 (10, 11) sts at beginning of next 4 rows. Divide remaining 44 (48, 50) sts in half and transfer each half to a spare needle or stitch holder.

Join fronts to back at shoulders.

FRONT BANDS

Right front
With 2¾mm needles and yarn A, beginning at lower edge, pick up and knit 89 (93, 97) sts up front opening edge as far as start of neck shaping; then pick up 88 (92, 97) sts around the neck edge to centre-back, including the 22 (24, 25) sts on the first spare needle. Work 3 rows in k1, p1 twisted rib in yarn A.
Buttonholes: Make five buttonholes in the 4th row of ribbing as follows: rib 4 sts, *cast off 3, rib 17 (18, 19); repeat from * 3 more times, cast off 3 sts and rib to end. Then rib back across the next row, casting on 3 sts directly over those cast off in previous row. Work 4 more rows in rib in yarn A; then work one row in rib in yarn B. Cast off in rib in yarn B.

Left front
Beginning at the centre-back, with yarn A, rib the 22 (24, 25) sts on the spare needle and then pick up and knit 66 (68, 72) sts around neck edge to start of neck shaping, then 89 (93, 97) sts down front to lower edge. Work to correspond with right front band, omitting buttonholes.

ARMHOLE BANDS

With 2¾mm needles and yarn A, pick up and knit 148 (154, 160) sts around one armhole. Work to correspond with left front band in k1, p1 twisted rib. Repeat for other armhole.

POCKETS

Pocket tops
With 2¾mm needles and yarn A, rib across the 28 (32, 36) sts of one pocket on the spare needle. Work to correspond with left front band.

TO MAKE UP

Press Fair Isle pieces lightly from wrong side, avoiding ribbing. Join fronts to back at sides. Join ribbing at back of neck. Sew down the sides of pocket tops and sew the three sides of each pocket lining to the wrong side of waistcoat fronts. Sew buttons to left front band. Press seams lightly from wrong side.

PURPLE PANSY

*Warm and loose-fitting, this long one-size sweater
can be worn as a sweater dress. The neck is worked in silver lurex yarn
for a more decorative effect.*

MATERIALS

Yarn

Use a 2-ply jumper weight Shetland yarn
unless otherwise indicated.

Yarn A 75g *(ivory)*
Yarn B 75g *(purple)*
Yarn C 100g *(oat)*
Yarn D 50g *(yellow)*
Yarn E 50g *(clan green)*
Yarn F 25g *(pale lilac mix)*
Yarn G 50g *(wine)*
Yarn H 50g *(wine mix)*
Yarn J 50g *(bluebell)*
Yarn K 50g *(navy)*
Yarn L 75g *(violet)*
Yarn M 100g mohair *(white)*
Yarn N 75g lurex *(silver)*

Needles

1 pair size 3¼mm
1 pair size 2¾mm
1 circular needle, size 2¾mm

MEASUREMENTS

One-size; to fit chest 86–97cm
(34–38in).
(See also chart on p. 118.)

Tension

31 sts and 31 rows measure 10cm over
Fair Isle pattern on 3¼mm needles.

BACK

With 2¾mm needles and yarn N, cast on
156 sts. Work 1 row in k1, p1 twisted rib
in yarn N. Join in yarn A and continue in
twisted rib for 5cm in yarn A.
Change to 3¼mm needles and st st and
work Pansy pattern from chart, reading
odd (knit) rows from right to left and even
(purl) rows from left to right. Repeat the
basic 16 pattern sts (*1–16*) indicated on
chart nine times across the row and work
the extra 12 sts (*17–28*) at the end of knit
and at the beginning of purl rows. Work
rows 1–20 inclusive from chart. Then
work rows 21–26 in reversed st st in yarn
M as follows: row 21, knit; row 22, knit;
row 23, purl; row 24, knit; row 25, purl;
row 26, knit. Continue in pattern from
rows 27–46 and then work rows 47–52 in
yarn M in reversed st st as follows: row
47, purl; row 48, purl; row 49, knit; row
50, purl; row 51, knit; row 52, purl. You
have now completed the 52 rows of the
pattern chart. Continue repeating the
pattern chart until you have worked row
40 of the third working of the chart and
the back measures approximately 51cm
from the cast-on edge.

Shape armhole: Continuing in pattern, shape raglan edge as follows: cast off 5 sts at the beginning of the next 2 rows. *Decrease one st at each end of the next 3 rows; work one row straight.* Repeat from * to * sixteen more times – 70 rows in all. Cast off the remaining 44 sts (4 complete patterns and 6 rows of the fifth should have been worked in all).

FRONT

Work as for back until beginning of armhole shaping, casting on 156 sts and working to the end of row 40 of the third working of the pattern chart.

Shape armhole: Continuing in pattern, shape raglan edge as follows: cast off 5 sts at the beginning of the next 2 rows. *Decrease one st at each end of the next 3 rows; work one row straight. Repeat from * 10 more times – 86 sts. Then decrease one st at each end of the next 2 rows – 82 sts.

Shape neck: Continuing in pattern (row 36 of the fourth working of the pattern chart), shape neck as follows, *at the same time* continuing to shape raglan edge:

Row 1: K2 tog, k47 sts, turn. Put remaining sts on to a spare needle.
Row 2: Cast off 16 sts, purl to end (32 sts).
Row 3: K2 tog, knit to end.
Row 4: Cast off 4 sts, purl to last 2 sts, p2 tog.
Row 5: K2 tog, knit to end.
Row 6: Cast off 4 sts, purl to end.
Row 7: K2 tog, knit to end.
Row 8: Cast off 2 sts, purl to last 2 sts, p2 tog.
Row 9: K2 tog, knit to end.
Row 10: Cast off 2 sts, purl to end.
Row 11: K2 tog, knit to end.
Row 12: Cast off 2 sts, purl to last 2 sts, p2 tog.
Row 13: K2 tog, knit to end.
Row 14: Cast off 2 sts, purl to end.
Row 15: K2 tog, knit to end.
Row 16: Cast off 2 sts, purl to end.
Row 17: K2 tog, knit to end.
Row 18: Cast off 2 sts. Fasten off.
Rejoin wool at neck edge. Work other side of neck to match, reversing all shapings at neck edge and raglan edge.

SLEEVES

Right sleeve

With 2¾mm needles and yarn N, cast on 66 sts. Work one row in k1, p1 twisted rib in yarn N. Change to yarn A and continue in twisted rib for 8cm, increasing across the last wrong-side row as follows: rib 8 sts, *make one st, rib 2 sts; repeat from * across row to the last 8 sts; make one st, rib 8 sts – 92 sts.

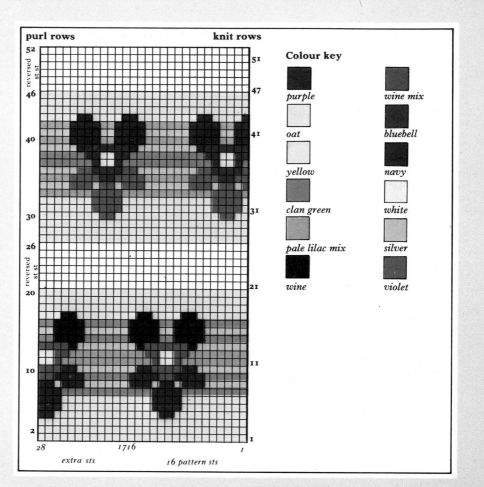

purl rows   **knit rows**

Colour key

purple   wine mix
oat   bluebell
yellow   navy
clan green   white
pale lilac mix silver
wine   violet

28   1716   1
extra sts   16 pattern sts

Change to 3¼mm needles and st st and work Pansy pattern from chart repeating sts *1–16* five times across the row and working sts *17–28* at the end of the row on knit rows; work purl rows in reverse. Increase one st at each end of the 7th and every following 6th row, 20 times in all, taking the extra sts into the pattern as they are made – 132 sts after 121 rows. Then work straight until you have completed row 40 of the third working of the pattern chart and the sleeve measures approximately 54cm from the cast-on edge.

Shape sleeve top: Continuing in pattern, cast off 6 sts at the beginning of the next 2 rows. *Decrease one st at each end of the next 3 rows. Work one row straight. Repeat from * thirteen more times – 36 sts. Then decrease one st at each end of the next 2 rows** – 32 sts. With right side of work facing starting at row 49 of the fourth working of the pattern chart, shape the top of the sleeve over the next 10 rows as follows:

Row 1: Cast off 11 sts; knit to end.
Row 2: P2 tog, purl to end.
Row 3: Cast off 5 sts, knit to last 2 sts, k2 tog.
Row 4: P2 tog, purl to end.
Row 5: Cast off 3 sts, knit to end.
Row 6: P2 tog, purl to end.
Row 7: Cast off 2 sts, knit to last 2 sts, k2 tog.
Row 8: P2 tog, purl to end – 5 sts.
Row 9: Cast off 2 sts, knit to end.
Row 10: P2 tog, p1: cast off.

Left sleeve

Work as for right sleeve to ** (32 sts).
Shape top of sleeve: With right side facing, starting at row 49 of the fourth working of chart, shape top of the left sleeve as follows:

Row 1: Knit to end.
Row 2: Cast off 11 sts, purl to last 2 sts, p2 tog.
Row 3: K2 tog, knit to end.
Row 4: Cast off 5 sts, purl to last 2 sts, p2 tog.
Row 5: Knit to end.
Row 6: Cast off 3 sts, purl to last 2 sts, p2 tog.
Row 7: K2 tog, knit to end.
Row 8: Cast off 2 sts, purl to last 2 sts, p2 tog.
Row 9: Knit to end (5 sts).
Row 10: Cast off 2 sts, purl one st, p2 tog. Cast off.

NECKBAND

Join sleeves to front and back at raglan edges. Using the circular 2¾mm needles and yarn N, with right side of the work facing, pick up and knit 176 sts around neck edge. Work 8 rounds in k1, p1 twisted rib in yarn N. Cast off in rib.

TO MAKE UP

Press pieces lightly on wrong side, avoiding ribbing. Join underarm seams of sleeves and side seams. Press seams.

ROSES

Romantic Roses in pink and blue on an écru ground
broken up with bands of grey Turkish stitch
form the pattern for this pretty cotton cardigan.

MATERIALS

Yarn
Use No. 8 cotton yarn.
Yarn A 250g *(écru)*
Yarn B 150g *(grey)*
Yarn C 50g *(pale blue)*
Yarn D 50g *(mid-blue)*
Yarn E 50g *(brown)*
Yarn F 50g *(pink)*
Yarn G 50g *(deep pink)*

Needles
1 pair size 3¼mm
1 pair size 2¾mm

Notions
8 buttons
1m hat elastic

MEASUREMENTS

To fit bust 86–89 (91–94)cm (34–35, 36–37in).
(See also chart on p. 118.)

Tension
32 sts and 38 rows measure 10cm over Rose pattern on 3¼mm needles.

BACK

With 2¾mm needles and yarn A, cast on 124 (134) sts. Work 5cm in k1, p1 twisted rib in yarn A, increasing across the last (wrong-side) row as follows: rib 2 (4) sts, *rib 3 sts, rib twice into the next st, rib 2 (3) sts; repeat from * 19 (17) times, rib 2 (4) sts – 144 (152) sts.
Change to 3¼mm needles and st st and work Rose pattern from chart, reading odd (knit) rows from right to left and even (purl) rows from left to right. Work the pattern across knit rows as follows: *for the small size,* work sts 1–12, twelve times; *for the large size,* work sts 1–12, twelve times and then work sts 1–8 once to finish row. Work purl rows in reverse. Continue thus in the pattern until you have worked row 14 of the chart. Then work rows 15–24 inclusive in Turkish st in yarn B as follows: k1, *yfwd, slip 1, k1, psso; repeat from * to last st, k1. Repeat this row nine times more. Then work rows 25–38 of the chart in st st in pattern and work rows 39–48 in Turkish st as for rows 15–24. You have now completed the 48 rows of the pattern chart. Continue in pattern until you have worked row 24 (28) of third working of chart and back measures approx. 37 (38)cm from cast-on edge.
Shape armholes: Continuing in pattern, cast off 10 (12) sts at the beginning of the next 2 rows – 124 (128) sts. Then work straight until you have worked row 8 (16) of the fifth working of the pattern chart and front measures 57 (59)cm from cast-on edge.
Shape shoulders: Continuing in pattern, cast off 13 (14) sts at the beginning of the

next 4 rows. Then cast off 12 sts at the beginning of the following 2 rows. Cast off the remaining 48 sts.

FRONTS

Left front
With 2¾mm needles and yarn A, cast on 58 (62) sts. Work 5cm in k1, p1 twisted rib in yarn A, increasing across the last wrong-side row as follows: rib 5 (1) sts, *rib 2 sts, rib twice into the next st, rib 2 (3) sts; repeat from * 9 more times, rib 3 (1) sts – 68 (72) sts.
Change to 3¼mm needles and st st and work pattern from chart. Work pattern across knit rows as follows: *for the small size,* repeat sts 1–12 five times across row and then work sts 1–8 once; *for the large size,* repeat sts 1–12 six times across the rows. Work purl rows in reverse. Continue thus in pattern until you have worked row 24 (28) of the third working of the pattern chart and front measures approximately 37 (38)cm from cast-on edge.
Shape armhole: Continuing in pattern, cast off 10 (12) sts at the beginning of the next row – 58 (60) sts. Then work straight in pattern until you have worked row 29 (37) of the fourth working of the pattern chart and the armhole measures approximately 13 (14)cm from the start of the armhole shaping.
Shape neck: Continuing in pattern, cast off 4 sts at the beginning of the next (wrong-side) row. Then decrease one st at the neck edge on every row until 38 (40) sts remain. Now work straight in pattern until you have worked row 8 (16) of the fifth working of the chart.
Shape shoulder: Cast off 13 (14) sts at the beginning of the next and following alternate row; then cast off 12 sts at the beginning of the following alternate row.

Right front
Work as for left front, reversing all shapings.

SLEEVES

With 2¾mm needles and yarn A, cast on 56 (60) sts. Work 10 (11)cm in twisted rib in yarn A, increasing across the last (wrong-side) row as follows: rib 8 (10) sts, *rib one st, rib twice into the next st; repeat from * 19 more times, rib 8 (10) sts – 76 (80) sts.
Change to 3¼mm needles and st st and work pattern from chart as follows: *for the small size,* repeat sts 1–12 six times and then work sts 1–4 once to complete the row; *for the large size,* repeat sts 1–12 six times and then work sts 1–8 once to complete row. Work purl rows in reverse. Continue in pattern, *at the same time*

shaping the sides by increasing one st each end of the 3rd and every following 4th row, until there are 130 (136) sts on the needle. Take the extra sts into the pattern as they are made. Then work straight in pattern until you have worked row 20 (24) of the fourth working of the pattern chart and the sleeve measures approximately 53 (55)cm from the cast-on edge. Cast off right across row; this cast-off edge should measure 41 (43)cm to fit armhole.

FRONT BANDS

Left front
With 2¾mm needles and yarn A, beginning at the start of the neck shaping with right side facing, pick up and knit 155 (162) sts down left front opening edge to lower edge. Work 9 rows of twisted rib in yarn A. Join in yarn B and work a further row in rib in yarn B, then cast off.

Right front
Starting at lower edge, pick up and knit 155 (162) sts up right front opening edge

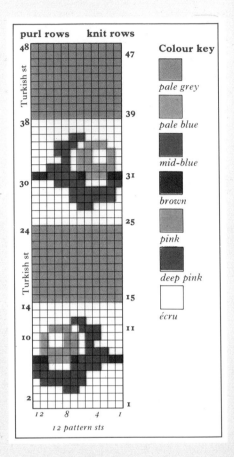

purl rows   knit rows

Turkish st

Turkish st

12 pattern sts

Colour key

pale grey

pale blue

mid-blue

brown

pink

deep pink

écru

as far as start of neck shaping. Work 3 rows in twisted rib in yarn A.

Buttonholes: Make 8 buttonholes in row 4 of ribbing as follows: rib 3 sts, *cast off 3 sts, rib 18 (19) sts; repeat from * six more times, then cast off 3 sts, rib 2 sts. Rib back along the next row (row 5), casting on 3 sts directly over those cast off in previous row. Work 4 more rows in rib in yarn A. Join in yarn B and work a further row in rib in yarn B. Cast off in rib in yarn B.

COLLAR

With 2¾mm needles and yarn A, cast on 109 (113) sts. Work one row in twisted rib. Continuing in twisted rib, increase one st at each end of the next and following 5 alternative rows. Then increase one st at each end of the following 6 rows – 133 (137) sts. Then work 4 (6) rows straight in rib. Now decrease one st at each end of the next 6 rows, and then decrease one st at each end of the following 6 alternate rows – 109 (113) sts. Work one row straight in rib. Cast off in rib.

TO MAKE UP

Press pieces lightly from wrong side, avoiding ribbing and Turkish st bands. Join shoulder seams and side seams. Join underarm sleeve seams, leaving 4 (5)cm of the seam unstitched at the top of the seam. Pin the top of the sleeve into the top of the armhole, easing if necessary, and then pin each side of the unstitched section of sleeve seam across the straight cast-off edge at the bottom of the armhole. Sew sleeve in place and repeat for other sleeve. Pin cast-on edge of collar around neck edge, aligning it between inner cast-on edges of front bands. Sew in position and then fold the collar in half so that the cast-off edge just overlaps this seam on inside of cardigan. Pin this edge in position and sew down neatly. Sew buttons on to left front band to correspond with buttonholes. Cut the hat elastic to fit around top of hips and thread this length through the bottom of the welt from the wrong side, securing ends. Press seams lightly from wrong side.

DAISY

*White and yellow Daisies against a soft grey background,
broken up with bands of mohair. The waistcoat back
is worked in striped rib and the beret is worked in the round.*

MATERIALS Hat

Yarn
Use 2-ply jumper weight Shetland yarn
unless otherwise indicated.
Yarn A 50g *(pale grey mix)*
Yarn B 25g *(ivory)*
Yarn C 25g *(yellow)*
Yarn D 25g *(dark grey mix)*
Yarn E 25g *(peat)*
Yarn F 25g *(sage green)*
Yarn G 50g lurex *(silver)*
Yarn H 25g mohair *(pale grey)*

Needles
1 set of four *or* circular size 3¼mm
1 set of four *or* circular size 2¾mm

MEASUREMENTS
One-size; to fit an average head.
(See also chart on p. 118.)

Tension
32 sts and 32 rows measure 10cm over
Fair Isle pattern on 3¼mm needles.

Headband
With 2¾mm needles and yarn A, cast on
160 sts (i.e. 53 sts on each of two needles
and 54 on the third, if using four needles).
Work band in rounds of k1, p1 twisted rib
in the following three-colour stripe
sequence:
Round 1: Yarn D
Round 2: Yarn G
Round 3: Yarn A
Repeat rounds 1–3 for 11cm, ending with
a round in yarn G. Increase around the
next round as follows: (yarn A) *k1, knit
twice into the next st; repeat from * all
round – 240 sts.

Crown
Change to 3¼mm needles or the circular
3¼mm needle and st st and work Daisy
pattern from chart, reading *every* row from
right to left and *knitting* every row as you
are working in rounds. Repeat the 16
pattern sts fifteen times across round and
work rows 1–21. Change to yarn H and
work 6 rounds in *purl*. Turn back to chart,
and work from row 28 to the end of row 48
in knit as before. Then purl 6 rounds in
yarn H.

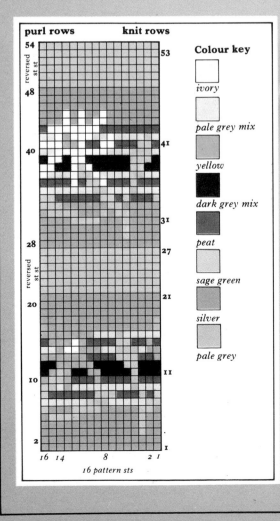

purl rows | **knit rows**

54 — 53
reversed st st
48

41

40

31

28 | 27

reversed st st
21

20

11

10

2 — 1

16 14   8   2 1

16 pattern sts

Colour key
□ ivory
□ pale grey mix
■ yellow
■ dark grey mix
■ peat
■ sage green
□ silver
□ pale grey

Shape crown: Change back to the three-colour stripe sequence of yarns D, G and A used for headband and decrease for crown as follows:
Round 1: (Yarn D) *k8, slip 1, k1, pass slipped st over (psso); repeat from * all round – 216 sts.
Rounds 2 and 3: (Yarns G and A) Work straight.
Round 4: (Yarn D) *k7, slip 1, k1, psso; repeat from * all round – 192 sts.
Rounds 5 and 6: (Yarns G and A) Work straight.
Round 7: (Yarn D) *k6, slip 1, k1, psso; repeat from * all round – 168 sts.
Rounds 8 and 9: (Yarns G and A) Work straight.
Continue decreasing in this way, decreasing 24 sts in each decrease round and working 2 rounds straight in between, until you have worked the round: *k1, slip 1, k1, psso; repeat from * all round – 48 sts. Work 2 more rounds straight. **On the next round, k2 tog all round – 24 sts. Work 2 rounds straight. Repeat from ** 2 more times – 6 sts. Break yarn leaving about a 15cm end. Thread this end through the 6 sts; draw up and secure.

TO MAKE UP

Fold headband in half to inside and pin inner edge in position. Slip stitch this edge to main body of hat. Darn in any loose ends. Press hat flat at first round of mohair to give tam o'shanter shape.

MATERIALS Waistcoat

Yarn
Use 2-ply jumper weight Shetland yarn.
Yarn A 100g *(pale grey mix)*
Yarn B 25g *(ivory)*
Yarn C 25g *(yellow)*
Yarn D 25g *(dark grey mix)*
Yarn E 50g *(peat)*
Yarn F 25g *(sage green)*
Yarn G 25g lurex *(silver)*
Yarn H 25g mohair *(pale grey)*
Needles
1 pair size 3¼mm
1 pair size 3mm
1 pair size 2¾mm
Notions
5 buttons

MEASUREMENTS

To fit chest 84 (91, 99)cm (33, 36, 39in). *(See also chart on p. 118.)*
Tension
32 sts and 32 rows measure 10cm over Fair Isle pattern on 3¼mm needles.

FRONTS

Pocket linings
Begin by making both pocket linings as follows: with 3mm needles and yarn A, cast on 28 (32, 36) sts and work 7cm in st st, ending with a purl row. Leave sts on a spare needle or stitch holder. Repeat for other pocket lining.

Left front
With 2¾mm needles and yarn A, cast on 66 (72, 78) sts. Work 5cm in k1, p1 twisted rib in yarn A.
Change to 3¼mm needles and st st and work Daisy pattern from chart, reading odd (knit) rows from right to left and even (purl) rows from left to right. Work the pattern across the rows as follows: *for the small size* (84cm), work sts *1–16* four times and then work sts *1–2* once; *for the medium size* (91cm), work sts *1–16* four times, then work sts *1–8* once; *for the large size* (99cm), work sts *1–16* four times, then work sts *1–14* once. Work purl rows in reverse, working the extra sts at the beginning of the rows and reading from left to right. Continue in pattern, until you have worked row 20 of the pattern chart.

Pocket: Introduce pocket in row 21 as follows: continuing in pattern, work the pattern across the first 19 (20, 21) sts in the row, then slip the next 28 (32, 36) sts on to a spare needle or stitch holder and in their place continue to work the pattern across the 28 (32, 36) sts of one pocket

lining on spare needle; then work pattern across remaining 19 (20, 21) sts in row. Work the next 6 rows in reversed st st in yarn H as follows: row 22, purl; row 23, purl; row 24, knit; row 25, purl; row 26, knit; row 27, knit.
Then work Daisy pattern again from row 28 to the end of row 48. Work the next 6 rows in reversed st st in yarn H as follows: row 49, knit; row 50, knit; row 51, purl; row 52, knit; row 53, purl; row 54, knit. You have now completed the 54 rows of the first working of the pattern chart. Continue in pattern until you have worked row 26 (30, 34) of the second working of chart and front measures approximately 30 (31, 32)cm from cast-on edge.
Shape armhole and neck: Cast off 10 (12, 14) sts at the beginning of the next row, then work across row in pattern to the last 2 sts; k2 tog. Continuing in pattern, decrease one st at the armhole edge on the next 14 (15, 16) rows. Then work armhole edge straight. *At the same time*, continue to decrease one st at the neck edge on every following 4th row after the first decrease on row 27 (31, 35), until 26 (28, 30) sts remain on the needle. Then work neck edge straight until you have completed row 36 (44, 52) of the third working of the pattern chart and front measures approximately 50 (52, 53)cm from the cast-on edge.
Shape shoulder: Cast off 8 (8, 10) sts at the beginning of the next (right-side) row. Then cast off 9 (10, 10) sts at the beginning of the following 2 alternate rows.

Right front
Work as for left front, but reverse pocket, armhole, neck and shoulder shapings.

BACK

With 2¾mm needles and yarn A, cast on 128 (140, 152) sts. Work 5cm in k1, p1 twisted rib in yarn A, increasing 4 sts evenly across the last wrong-side row by working twice into every 32nd (35th, 38th) st, 4 times – 132 (144, 156) sts.

back of waistcoat

55

DAISY

Change to 3mm needles and continue to work entire back in twisted rib in the following three-colour stripe sequence:
Row 1: Yarn D
Row 2: Yarn E
Row 3: Yarn A
Repeat rows 1–3 up back without shaping until work measures approximately 30 (31, 32)cm from cast-on edge and matches the fronts from cast-on edge to start of armhole shaping, ending on a wrong-side row.
Shape armholes: Cast off 3 (4, 6) sts at the beginning of the next 2 rows, then k2 tog at each end of every row until 100 (104, 108) sts remain. Then work armhole edges straight until the back measures the same as the fronts from cast-on edge to start of shoulder shaping – approximately 50 (52, 53)cm – ending on a wrong-side row.
Shape shoulders: Cast off 8 (8, 10) sts at the beginning of the next 2 rows. Then cast off 9 (10, 10) sts at the beginning of the following 4 rows. Divide the remaining 48 (50, 52) sts in half and transfer each half to a spare needle or stitch holder.

Join fronts to back at shoulders.

FRONT BANDS

Right front
With 2¾mm needles and yarn A, beginning at hem edge and with right side of work facing, pick up and knit 93 (97, 101) sts up right front opening edge, as far as start of neck shaping; then pick up and knit a further 89 (93, 97) sts around the neck to the centre-back, including the 24 (25, 26) sts on the first spare needle – 182 (190, 198) sts in all. Work 3 rows in k1, p1 twisted rib in yarn A.
Buttonholes: Make 5 buttonholes in the 4th row as follows: rib 4 sts, *cast off 3 sts, rib 18 (19, 20) sts; repeat from * 3 more times, cast off 3 sts and rib to end of row. Rib back along the next row (5th row of ribbing), casting on 3 sts directly over those cast off in the previous row. Work a further 4 rows in twisted rib in yarn A. Then join in yarn D and work one row twisted rib in yarn D. Cast off in rib in yarn D.

Left front
With 2¾mm needles and yarn A, beginning at the centre-back of the neck and with right side facing rib the 24 (25, 26) sts on the remaining spare needle, then pick up and knit 65 (68, 71) sts round neck edge to start of neck shaping; then pick up and knit 93 (97, 101) sts down front opening edge to hem. Work to correspond with right front band, omitting buttonholes.

ARMHOLE BANDS

With right side facing, using 2¾mm needles and yarn A, pick up and knit 144 (152, 160) sts around one armhole. Work 9 rows in k1, p1 twisted rib in yarn A. Join in yarn D and work a further row in rib in yarn D. Cast off in rib in yarn D. Repeat for other armhole.

POCKET TOPS

With right side facing, using 2¾mm needles and yarn A, rib the 28 (32, 36) sts of one pocket on spare needle. Work to correspond with left front band. Repeat for other pocket.

TO MAKE UP

Press all pieces lightly from the wrong side, avoiding ribbing. Join side seams. Join ribbing at back of neck with a flat seam. Sew down sides of pocket tops and sew pocket linings to backs of waistcoat fronts. Sew on five buttons to left front band to correspond with buttonholes.

MATERIALS

Yarn
Use No. 8 cotton yarn.
Yarn A 100g (*écru*)
Yarn B 50g (*purple*)
Yarn C 50g (*bluebell*)
Yarn D 50g (*pale green*)
Yarn E 50g (*pink*)
Yarn F 50g (*deep pink*)
Yarn G 50g (*beige*)
Needles
1 pair size 3¼mm
1 pair size 2¼mm
Notions
1m shirring or hat elastic

MEASUREMENTS

To fit bust 86 (91)cm (34, 36in).
(*See also chart on p. 119.*)
Tension
32 sts and 32 rows measure 10cm over Fair Isle pattern on 3¼mm needles.

BACK and FRONT

Work the back and the front in the same way.
With 2¼mm needles and yarn A, cast on 120 (126) sts. Work 5 (6)cm in k1, p1 twisted rib.
Change to 3¼mm needles and st st and work Sweet pea pattern from chart, reading odd (knit) rows from right to left and even (purl) rows from left to right. Work the pattern across the rows as follows: *for the smaller size* (86cm), repeat the basic 14 pattern sts (*1–14*), eight times across the row and then work sts 1–8 once to finish the row; *for the larger size* (91cm), work sts 1–14, nine times across the row. Work purl rows in reverse. Continue thus until you have worked row 14 of the pattern chart. Then work the next 10 rows in Turkish st in yarn A only as follows (see also p. 130): k1, *yfwd, slip 1, k1, psso; repeat from * to last st, k1. Work rows 16–24 inclusive in the same way as row 15. Then work rows 25–38 in Sweet pea pattern from chart and rows 39–48 in Turkish st in the same way as rows 15–24. You have now completed the 48 rows of the first working of the pattern chart. Work rows 1–38 of pattern chart again. Change to 2¼mm needles and work 5cm in k1, p1 twisted rib in yarn A, ending with a wrong-side row, to form top welt. Join in yarn C and work another row in twisted rib. Cast off in rib in yarn C.

SHOULDER STRAPS

With 2¼mm needles and yarn A, cast on 112 (116) sts. Work 3cm in k1, p1 twisted rib in yarn A. Then cast off in rib in yarn A. Make another strap in the same way.

SWEET PEAS

*Pretty pink and purple Sweet peas are worked in bands
against an écru ground in this close-fitting cotton summer camisole.
Bands of Turkish stitch separate the pattern.*

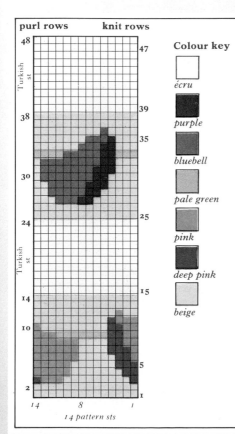

purl rows   **knit rows**

Colour key

- □ *écru*
- ■ *purple*
- ■ *bluebell*
- ■ *pale green*
- ■ *pink*
- ■ *deep pink*
- □ *beige*

14 pattern sts

TO MAKE UP

Press front and back pieces lightly from
the wrong side, avoiding ribbing. Join
front to back at side seams. Measure 5cm
in from side seams at top ribbing on front
and back and mark each point with a pin.
Align straps with these points, pin in
position, adjust if necessary. Sew each
strap in position, just below the edging.
Press seams from wrong side. Cut the
length of shirring or hat elastic to fit
waist and thread it through the bottom
edge of the hem welt from the wrong side,
taking care that it does not show through
on the right side, securing it firmly at
side seam.

PRETTY PANSIES

*Delicate pink and purple Pansies on an ivory ground
with bands of white mohair running in between the pattern.
The cardigan has three-quarter length sleeves pleated into the armholes.*

MATERIALS

Yarn
Use 2-ply jumper weight Shetland yarn
unless otherwise indicated.
Yarn A 125g *(ivory)*
Yarn B 25g *(pale yellow)*
Yarn C 25g *(pale lilac mix)*
Yarn D 25g *(powder blue)*
Yarn E 25g *(wine mix)*
Yarn F 25g *(lilac/green mix)*
Yarn G 25g *(clan green)*
Yarn H 25g *(pale pink mix)*
Yarn J 100g mohair *(white)*
Yarn K 25g lurex *(silver)*

Needles
1 pair size 3¼mm
1 pair size 3mm
1 pair size 2¼mm

Notions
5 pearl buttons

MEASUREMENTS

One-size: to fit bust 86–91cm (34–36in).
(See also chart on p. 119.)

Tension
30 sts and 30 rows measure 10cm over
Fair Isle pattern on 3¼mm needles.

BACK

With 2¼mm needles and yarn A, cast on
128 sts. Work 5cm in k1, p1 twisted rib,
increasing on the last wrong-side row as
follows: *rib 7, rib twice into the next st;
repeat from * 16 more times – 144 sts.
Change to 3¼mm needles and st st and
work Pansy pattern from chart, reading
odd (knit) rows from right to left and even
(purl) rows from left to right. Repeat the
16 pattern sts nine times across the rows.
Continue in pattern until you have worked
row 20 of the pattern chart. Change to
yarn J (mohair) and work 6 rows of
reverse st st as follows: row 21, knit; row
22, knit; row 23, purl; row 24, knit; row
25, purl; row 26, knit. Then continue to
work pattern from chart from row 27,
until you have worked row 46.
Change to yarn J again and work rows
47–52 as for rows 21–26. You have now
completed the first working of the pattern
chart. Continue to work pattern, until
you have worked row 22 of the second
working of the pattern chart, and the
back measures approximately 29cm from
cast-on edge.
Shape armholes: Continuing in pattern,
cast off 8 sts at the beginning of the next 2
rows (rows 23 and 24). Then k2 tog at
each end of every row until 108 sts remain.
Now work straight until you have worked
row 34 of the third working of the pattern
chart and the back measures approximately 51cm.
Shape shoulders: Continuing in pattern,

cast off 6 sts at the beginning of the next
and following 3 rows. Then cast off 7 sts
at the beginning of the next 6 rows.
Divide the remaining 42 sts in half and
transfer each half to a spare needle or
stitch holder.

FRONTS

Pocket linings
Begin by making two pocket linings. With
3mm needles and yarn A, cast on 28 sts.
Work 6cm in st st in yarn A, ending with
a purl row. Leave sts on spare needle.
Repeat for other pocket lining.

Left front
With 2¼mm needles and yarn A, cast on
56 sts. Work 5cm in k1, p1 twisted rib in
yarn A, increasing across the last (wrong-
side) row as follows: *rib 3 sts, rib twice
into the next st, rib 3 sts; repeat from *
seven more times – 64 sts.
Change to 3¼mm needles and st st and
work Pansy pattern from chart as before,
repeating the 16 pattern sts four times
across each row. Continue in pattern until
you have worked row 20 of pattern chart.
Pocket: Introduce pocket in the next row
(row 21) as follows: work the first 18 sts in
the row, slip the next 28 sts on to a spare
needle or stitch holder and in their place,
continue to work the pattern across the 28
sts of one pocket lining on spare needle;
work pattern across the remaining 18 sts
in the row. Continuing in pattern, work
the front straight until you have completed row 12 of the second working of the
pattern chart.
Shape neck and armhole edge: Continuing in pattern, work across the next
row to the last 2 sts; k2 tog. Then
decrease one st at the neck edge on every
following 5th row, thirteen times in all,
keeping in pattern. *At the same time,* when
you have completed row 22 of the second
working of the pattern chart and the front
measures approximately 29cm, shape
armhole as follows: cast off 8 sts at the
beginning of the next row (row 75). Then
decrease one st at the armhole edge on the
following 10 rows. Now work armhole
edge straight, but continue decreasing one
st at the neck edge on every 5th row until
33 sts remain. Then work straight in
pattern until you have completed row 34
of the third working of the pattern chart.
Shape shoulders: Cast off 6 sts at the
beginning of the next and following
alternate row. Then cast off 3 sts at the
beginning of the following 3 alternate rows.

Right front
Work as for left front, reversing pocket,
neck, armhole and shoulder shapings.

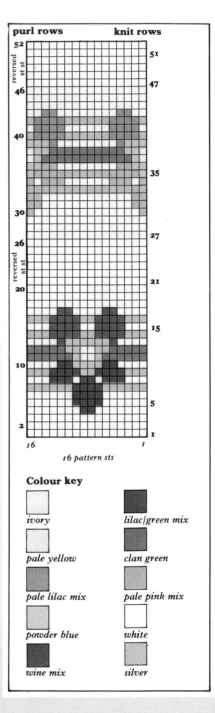

purl rows   knit rows

16 pattern sts

Colour key

ivory	lilac/green mix
pale yellow	clan green
pale lilac mix	pale pink mix
powder blue	white
wine mix	silver

SLEEVES

With 2¼mm needles and yarn G, cast on 66 sts and work one row in k1, p1 twisted rib in yarn G.

Join in yarn A and continue in rib for 7cm, increasing across the last (wrong-side) row as follows: rib 10 sts, rib twice into each of the next 46 sts, rib 10 sts – 112 sts in all.

Change to 3¼mm needles and st st and work straight in pattern from chart, repeating the 16 pattern sts seven times across the rows. Work from chart until you have completed row 22 of the second working of the pattern chart, and sleeve measures approximately 31cm.

Shape top: Continuing in pattern, cast off 8 sts at the beginning of the next 2 rows. Then k2 tog at each end of the next and every alternate row, until 76 sts remain on the needle. Work 17 rows straight in pattern. K2 tog at each end of the next and every following alternate row, seven times in all; then k2 tog at each end of the next 9 rows – 42 sts remain. Cast off remaining sts, taking every 10th and 11th st in row together. This wide sleeve top will be gathered into the armhole later. Make another sleeve in the same way.

Join fronts to back at shoulders.

FRONT BANDS

Right front

With 2¼mm needles and yarn A, beginning at lower edge, pick up and knit 89 sts up front opening edge to start of neck shaping; then pick up and knit a further 113 sts around neck to centre-back, including the 21 sts on the first spare needle. Work 3 rows in k1, p1 twisted rib in yarn A.

Buttonholes: Make 5 buttonholes in row 4 of ribbing as follows: rib 4 sts, *cast off 3 sts, rib 17 sts; repeat from * three more times, cast off 3 sts and rib to end of row. On the next row (row 5) rib back, casting on 3 sts directly over those cast off in previous row. Work 4 more rows of rib in yarn A. Join in yarn G, and work one row of rib in yarn G. Cast off in rib in yarn G.

Left front

Starting at the centre-back and with yarn A, rib the 21 sts on the remaining spare needle; then pick up and knit 89 sts around neck edge to start of neck shaping, and a further 89 sts down front opening to lower edge. Work left front band to correspond with right front band, but omit buttonholes.

POCKETS

Pocket tops

With right side of work facing, using 2¼mm needles and yarn A, rib across the 28 sts of one pocket on spare needle. Work 7 more rows in k1, p1 twisted rib in yarn A. Join in yarn G and work a further row in twisted rib in yarn G. Cast off in rib in yarn G. Repeat for other pocket.

TO MAKE UP

Press all pieces lightly from wrong side avoiding ribbing. Join fronts to back at side seams. Join sleeve seams. Pin sleeves into each armhole, pleating fullness around top of sleeve as you pin in position. Sew sleeves into armholes as before. Join front bands at centre-back of neck with flat seam. Sew down sides of pocket tops and pocket linings. Sew on the 5 buttons to left front band to correspond with buttonholes.

ETHNIC

CACTUS

Prickly Cacti against desert shades are the theme of this sleeveless men's or women's V-neck waistcoat. The back, welts, armholes and neckband are worked in striped rib.

MEASUREMENTS

To fit chest 89 (97, 104, 112)cm (35, 38, 41, 44in).
(See also chart on p. 119.)

Tension

32 sts and 32 rows measure 10cm over Cactus pattern on 3¼mm needles.

MATERIALS

Yarn

Use 2-ply jumper weight Shetland yarn. Different sizes require different quantities of main yarn.

Yarn A 75 (100, 100, 100)g *(clan green)*
Yarn B 75 (100, 100, 100)g *(bottle green)*
Yarn C 75g *(peat)*
Yarn D 50g *(pale green mix)*
Yarn E 75g *(dark fawn)*
Yarn F 50g *(oat)*
Yarn G 50g *(pale grey mix)*
Yarn H 25g *(mustard mix)*
Yarn J 25g *(blue/wine mix)*
Yarn K 25g *(red/blue mix)*

Needles

1 pair size 3¼mm
1 pair size 3mm
1 pair size 2¾mm

Colour key

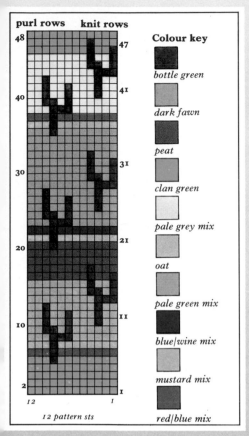

purl rows   knit rows

bottle green	
dark fawn	
peat	
clan green	
pale grey mix	
oat	
pale green mix	
blue/wine mix	
mustard mix	
red/blue mix	

12 pattern sts

next row straight. K2 tog at the beginning of the next row, then work to end. Work the next row straight. K2 tog at the beginning of the next row, work to last 2 sts, k2 tog**. Repeat from ** to ** until 33 (36, 41, 43) sts remain. Work the next row straight. K2 tog at the beginning of the next row, then work to end. Work the next row straight. Now work the armhole edge straight, but continue to decrease one st at the neck edge on the next and every following 4th row as before, until 24 (27, 30, 33) sts remain. Work straight in pattern until you have completed row 22 (30, 38, 46) of the fourth working of the pattern chart and the left front measures approximately 56 (59, 61, 64)cm from cast-on edge.
Shape shoulder: Continuing in pattern, cast off 8 (9, 10, 11) sts at the beginning of the next and following 2 alternate rows. Rejoin yarn to the remaining 59 (64, 69, 74) sts of front at neck edge. K2 tog at the beginning of the next row, then knit 55 (60, 65, 70) sts, k2 tog. **Work the next row straight. Work across the next row to the last 2 sts, k2 tog. Work the next row straight. K2 tog at the beginning of next row, work pattern to last 2 sts, k2 tog**. Repeat from ** to ** until 33 (36, 41, 43) sts remain. Finish right side to correspond with left side, reversing all shapings.

FRONT

With 2¾mm needles and yarn A, cast on 136 (148, 160, 172) sts. Work 5cm in k1, p1 twisted rib in the following three-colour stripe sequence:
Row 1: Yarn D
Row 2: Yarn C
Row 3: Yarn A
Continue repeating rows 1–3 for 5cm, ending with a row in yarn A. Change to yarn D and increase across this row as follows: purl 0 (2, 0, 2) sts, *purl twice into the next st, purl 16 (17, 19, 20) sts; repeat from * seven more times, purl 0 (2, 0, 2) sts – 144 (156, 168, 180) sts. Change to 3¼mm needles and st st and work pattern from chart, reading odd (knit) rows from right to left and even (purl) rows from left to right. Repeat the 12 pattern sts on chart, 12 (13, 14, 15) times across the row. Continuing in pattern, work straight until you have completed row 44 (48, 4, 8) of the second (second, third, third) working of the pattern chart and the front measures approximately 34 (35, 36, 37)cm from the cast-on edge.
Shape armholes and neck: Continuing in pattern, cast off 13 (14, 15, 16) sts at the beginning of the next 2 rows – 118 (128, 138, 148) sts remain. Now divide for 'V'-neck. On the next row, k2 tog, k55 (60, 65, 70) sts, k2 tog; then turn leaving the remaining sts in row on a spare needle or stitch holder. Now work the left side of the front on these 56 (61, 66, 71) sts as follows, continuing in pattern: **work the

BACK

With 2¾mm needles and yarn A, cast on 144 (156, 168, 180) sts. Work 5cm in k1, p1 twisted rib following the same three-colour stripe sequence as for front welt, ending with a row in yarn A.
Change to 3mm needles and continue to work entire back in striped twisted rib, repeating rows 1–3 and carrying yarns not in use up the sides of the work, until back measures approximately 34 (35, 36, 37)cm from cast-on edge, ending with a wrong-side row.
Shape armholes: Continuing in striped rib, cast off 8 (10, 12, 14) sts at the beginning of the next 2 rows. Then k2 tog at each end of the next and every following alternate row until 100 (108, 116, 124) sts remain. Now work straight until back measures approximately 56 (59, 61, 64)cm from the cast-on edge.
Shape shoulders: Continuing in striped rib, cast off 8 (9, 10, 11) sts at the beginning of the next 6 rows. Leave the remaining 52 (54, 56, 58) sts on a spare needle or stitch holder.

NECKBAND

Join right shoulder seam. With 2¾mm needles and yarn A, beginning at the left shoulder seam and with right side facing, pick up and knit 72 (76, 80, 84) sts down the side of the neck to centre and mark with coloured thread; then pick up 2 sts from the centre-front and mark again with coloured thread; pick up and knit 72 (76, 80, 84) sts up right side of neck and finally

knit the 52 (54, 56, 58) sts from the spare needle at the back of the neck. Work neckband in k1, p1 twisted rib in the same three-colour stripe sequence as before, shaping the neckband as follows: on the next row rib around back and down side of neck to last 2 sts before marker; slip 1, k1, psso, k2, k2 tog and then rib to end. On the next row, rib back down left side of neck to last 2 sts before marker, slip 1, k1, psso, k2, k2 tog, rib to end. Repeat these 2 rows three more times. Then cast off in rib in yarn A, still decreasing as before.

ARMBANDS

Join left shoulder seam and neckband. With right side facing, using 2¾mm needles and yarn A, pick up and knit 164 (170, 176, 182) sts around one armhole. Work 8 rows in twisted rib following the same three-colour stripe sequence as before. Cast off in rib in yarn A. Repeat for other armhole.

TO MAKE UP

Press front lightly from wrong side, avoiding ribbing. Join side seams and press seams lightly.

back of waistcoat

DOUBLE DUTCH

*A one-size crew neck sweater with patterned front and back
and plain sleeves. The pattern is derived from Delft tile designs.*

MATERIALS

Yarn
Use 2-ply jumper weight Shetland yarn.
Yarn A 225g *(navy)*
Yarn B 150g *(ivory)*
Yarn C 25g *(crimson)*
Needles
1 pair size 3¼mm
1 pair size 2¾mm

MEASUREMENTS

One-size: to fit chest 97cm (38in).
(See also chart on p. 119.)
Tension
30 sts and 30 rows measure 10cm over
Delft pattern on 3¼mm needles; 31 sts
and 32 rows measure 10cm over plain st st.

BACK

**With 2¾mm needles and yarn A, cast on
136 sts. Work 5cm in k1, p1 twisted rib in
yarn A. Increase across the next wrong-
side row as follows: rib 5 sts, *rib 5 sts,
rib twice into the next st; repeat from * 19
more times, rib 11 sts – 156 sts.
Change to 3¼mm needles and st st and
work Delft pattern from chart, reading
odd (knit) rows from right to left and even
(purl) rows from left to right. Repeat the
78 pattern sts indicated on chart, twice
across the row. Continue in pattern until
you have worked row 38 of the second
working of the pattern chart and the back
measures approximately 45cm from the
cast-on edge.**
Shape armholes: Cast off 12 sts at the
beginning of the next 2 rows. Then work
straight in pattern until you have worked
row 18 of the third working of the pattern
chart, and the work measures approximately 65cm from the cast-on edge.
Shape shoulders: With right side facing,
cast off 15 sts at the beginning of the next
2 rows. Then cast off 13 sts at the beginning of the next 4 rows. Leave the remaining 50 sts on a spare needle.

FRONT

Work front as for back from ** to **
completing row 38 of the second working
of the pattern chart.
Shape armholes: Cast off 12 sts at the
beginning of the next 2 rows – 132 sts.
Then work straight in pattern until you
have completed row 72 of the second
working of the pattern chart and the front
measures approximately 56cm from the
cast-on edge.
Shape neck: Work the first 48 sts of row
73 on chart, cast off the next 36 sts, and
then work the pattern across the remaining
48 sts of the row. Continuing in pattern on
these last 48 sts of the row, decrease one
st at the neck edge on the next 7 rows – 41
sts remain. Then work straight in pattern
until you have worked row 18 of the third
working of the pattern chart and the right
front shoulder edge measures approximately 65cm from the cast-on edge.

Shape shoulder: Continuing in pattern,
cast off 15 sts at the beginning of the next
row. Then cast off 13 sts at the beginning
of the following 2 alternate rows.
Rejoin yarn to the 48 sts of left front at
neck edge on spare needle. Work left side
of neck and left shoulder to correspond
with right side, reversing shapings.

SLEEVES

With 2¾mm needles and yarn A, cast on
62 sts. Work 10cm in k1, p1 twisted rib in
yarn A, ending on a right-side row.
Increase across the next (wrong-side) row
as follows: rib 10 sts, rib twice into each
of the next 42 sts, rib 10 sts – 104 sts in all.
Change to 3¼mm needles and knit one
row in yarn C. Rejoin yarn A and continue to work sleeve in st st and yarn A
only, starting with a purl row and shaping
sides by increasing one st at each end of
the next (after the purl row) and every
following 7th row until there are 132 sts
on the needle. Then work straight until
the sleeve measures 56cm from the cast-on
edge. Cast off right across row.
Make another sleeve in the same way.

NECKBAND

Join right shoulder seam only.
With right side of work facing, using
2¾mm needles and yarn A, beginning at
the left shoulder, pick up and knit 31 sts
down left side of neck, 30 sts across
centre-front cast-off edge, 31 sts up right
side of neck and 50 sts across back of neck
– 142 sts in all. Work 13 rows in k1, p1
twisted rib in yarn A. Join in yarn C and
work a further row of twisted rib in yarn
C. Cast off in rib in yarn C.

TO MAKE UP

Press all pieces lightly from the wrong
side avoiding ribbing. Join left shoulder
seam and neckband and both side seams.
Then join underarm sleeve seams, leaving
the last 4cm at top of seam unstitched.
Pin top of sleeve into top of armhole and
pin each side of the unstitched section of
the sleeve seam across the straight cast-off
edge at the bottom of the armhole. Sew
in place and repeat for other sleeve. Press
seams lightly from wrong side.

Colour key

navy   ivory

78 pattern sts

NAVAJO

An interesting pattern deriving from a Red Indian design,
using geometric shapes against a plain ground.
The back of the waistcoat is worked in plain rib.

MATERIALS

Yarn
Use 2-ply jumper weight Shetland yarn.
Different sizes will require different
quantities of main yarn.
Yarn A 125g (125g, 150g) *(oat)*
Yarn B 50g *(rust)*
Yarn C 50g *(black)*
Yarn D 25g *(mustard)*
Yarn E 25g *(lilac/green mix)*
Yarn F 25g *(olive mix)*
Needles
1 pair size 3¼mm
1 pair size 3mm
1 pair size 2¾mm
Notions
5 buttons

MEASUREMENTS

To fit chest 84 (91, 99)cm (33, 36, 39in).
(See also chart on p. 119.)
Tension
32 sts and 34 rows measure 10cm over
Fair Isle pattern on 3¼mm needles.

FRONTS

Left front
With 2¾mm needles and yarn A, cast on
66 (72, 78) sts. Work 5cm in k1, p1 twisted
rib in yarn A.
Change to 3¼mm needles and st st and
work Fair Isle pattern from chart, reading
odd (knit) rows from right to left and even
(purl) rows from left to right. Work the
pattern across knit rows as follows: *for the
small size* (84cm), work sts *1–40* once, then
work sts *1–26* once; *for the medium size*
(91cm), work sts *1–40* once, then work sts
1–32 once; *for the large size* (99cm), work
sts *1–40* once, then work sts *1–38* once.
Work purl rows in reverse. Continue in
pattern until the end of row 12 on chart.
Pocket: Introduce pocket in row 13
(right-side row) as follows: work the first
19 (20, 21) sts of row in pattern, cast off
the next 28 (32, 36) sts, and then continue
to work pattern to end of row. On the
next row, work the first 19 (20, 21) sts of
row in pattern, then cast on 28 (32, 36) sts
directly over those cast off and then work
pattern to end of row. Continue straight in
pattern until you have worked row 32 (36,
40) of the second working of the pattern
chart and the front measures approximately 32 (33, 35)cm from cast-on edge.
Shape armholes and neck: Cast off 10
(12, 14) sts at the beginning of the next
(right-side) row and then work the pattern
across row to the last 2 sts; k2 tog. Continuing in pattern, decrease one st at the
armhole edge on the next 14 (14, 16) rows,
and then work armhole edge straight. *At
the same time,* decrease one st at the neck
edge on every following 4th row after the

first decrease on row 33 (37, 41) until 26
(28, 30) sts remain. Then work neck edge
straight until you have worked row 48 (56,
62) of the third working of the pattern
chart and front measures approximately
55 (57, 60)cm from cast-on edge.
Shape shoulder: Continuing in pattern
(*for the larger size,* continue in plain st st
in yarn A only), cast off 10 sts at the
beginning of the next (right-side) row;
then cast off 8 (9, 10) sts at the beginning
of the following 2 alternate rows.

Right front
Work as for left front and reverse pocket,
armhole, neck and shoulder shapings.

BACK

With 2¾mm needles and yarn A, cast on
128 (140, 152) sts. Work 5cm in k1, p1
twisted rib, increasing to 132 (144, 156)
sts across the last (wrong-side) row by
working twice into every 32nd (35th, 38th)

st in the row, four times.
Change to 3mm needles and continue to
work entire back in twisted rib in yarn A.
Work until back measures same as front
from cast-on edge to start of armhole
shaping – approximately 32 (33, 35)cm –
ending on a wrong-side row.
Shape armholes: Cast off 4 (6, 8) sts at
the beginning of the next 2 rows. Then
k2 tog at each end of every row until 100
(106, 112) sts remain. Work straight until
back measures the same as the fronts from
cast-on edge to start of shoulder shaping –
approximately 55 (57, 60)cm – ending on
a wrong-side row.
Shape shoulders: With right side facing,
cast off 10 (11, 11) sts at the beginning of
the next 2 rows. Then cast off 9 (9, 10) sts
at the beginning of the following 4 rows.
Divide the remaining 44 (48, 50) sts in
half and transfer each half to a spare
needle or stitch holder.

Join fronts to back at shoulders.

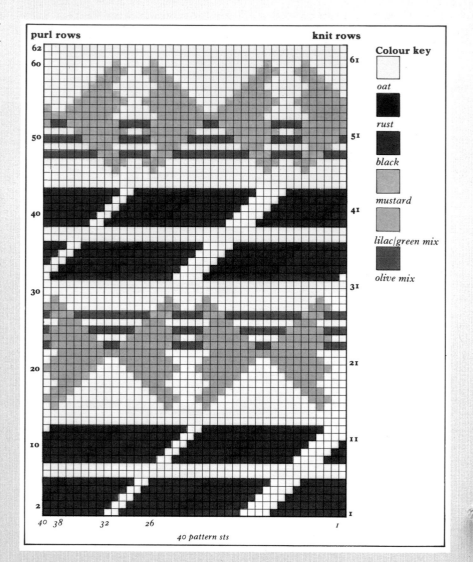

purl rows   knit rows

62   60   50   40   30   20   10   2

61   51   41   31   21   11   1

40   38   32   26   1

40 pattern sts

Colour key
oat
rust
black
mustard
lilac/green mix
olive mix

FRONT BANDS

Right front

With right side of the work facing and using 2¾mm needles and yarn A, beginning at hem edge, pick up and knit 97 (101, 105) sts up right front opening edge, as far as start of neck shaping; then pick up and knit a further 80 (84, 88) sts around neck opening edge as far as centre-back, including the 22 (24, 25) sts on the first spare needle – 177 (185, 193) sts in all. Work 3 rows in k1, p1 twisted rib in yarn A.

Buttonholes: Make five buttonholes in the next row (row 4) as follows: rib 4 sts, *cast off 3 sts, rib 19 (20, 21) sts; repeat from * 3 more times, then cast off 3 sts and rib to end of row. Rib back along next row, casting on 3 sts directly over those cast off in previous row. Work 4 more rows in rib in yarn A. Join in yarn C and work 1 row in rib in yarn C. Cast off in rib in yarn C.

Left front

Beginning at the centre-back of the neck, using 2¾mm needles and yarn A, rib the 22 (24, 25) sts on the remaining spare needle; then pick up and knit 58 (60, 63) sts around neck edge to start of neck shaping and then a further 97 (101, 105) sts down front opening edge to hem edge. Work to correspond with right front band, but omit buttonholes.

ARMHOLE BANDS

With 2¾mm needles and yarn A, and with right side of work facing, pick up and knit 147 (155, 163) sts around one armhole. Work to correspond with left front band. Repeat for other armhole.

POCKETS

Pocket tops

With right side of work facing and using 2¾mm needles and yarn A, pick up and knit 28 (32, 36) sts along the lower cast-off edge of one pocket slit. Work to correspond with left front band. Repeat for lower cast-off edge of other pocket slit.

Pocket linings

Holding work upside down and with right side facing, using 3mm needles and yarn A, pick up and knit 28 (32, 36) sts across the remaining cast-on edge of one pocket slit behind pocket top. Starting with a purl row, work in st st and yarn A, until the lining measures 7cm. Cast off. Repeat for other pocket.

TO MAKE UP

Press all pieces lightly from wrong side, avoiding ribbing. Join fronts to back at side seams. Join ribbing at centre-back of neck and underarm points with flat seams. Sew down pocket linings to wrong side of fronts and sew down sides of pocket tops. Sew on five buttons to left front band to correspond with buttonholes.

PIERROT

*Clownish colours speckled over alternating stripes make this
cotton cardigan an ideal summer garment. The cardigan buttons
to the neck and has a shaped, ribbed collar and front pockets.*

MATERIALS

Yarn
Use No. 8 cotton yarn.
Yarn A 250g *(écru)*
Yarn B 150g *(pale blue)*
Yarn C 50g *(lilac)*
Yarn D 50g *(bluebell)*
Yarn E 50g *(deep pink)*
Yarn F 50g *(yellow)*
Yarn G 50g *(purple)*

Needles
1 pair size 3¼mm
1 pair size 2¾mm

Notions
8 buttons
1m narrow hat elastic

MEASUREMENTS

To fit bust 86 (91)cm (34, 36in).
(See also chart on p. 120.)

Tension
32 sts and 32 rows measure 10cm over
Fair Isle pattern on 3¼mm needles.

BACK

With 2¾mm needles and yarn A, cast on
124 (134) sts. Work 5cm in k1, p1 twisted
rib, increasing across the last (wrong-side)
row as follows: rib 2 (4) sts, *rib 3 sts, rib
twice into the next st, rib 2 (3) sts; repeat
from * 19 (17) more times, rib 2 (4) sts –
144 (152) sts in all.
Change to 3¼mm needles and st st and
work pattern from chart, reading odd
(knit) rows from right to left and even
(purl) rows from left to right. Work the
pattern across knit rows as follows: *for the
smaller size (86cm)*, work the 24 pattern
sts (*1–24*), six times across the row; *for the
larger size (91cm)*, work sts *1–24* six times
across the row and then work sts *1–8* once
to finish the row. Work purl rows in
reverse, working sts *8–1* at the beginning
of the row for the larger size. Continuing
in pattern work straight until you have
completed row 12 (16) of the fourth working of the pattern chart and the back
measures approximately 31 (32)cm from
the cast-on edge.
Shape armholes: Continuing in pattern,
cast off 10 (13) sts at the beginning of the
next 2 rows – 124 (126) sts. Then work
straight until you have worked row 24 of
the sixth working of the pattern chart (row
8 of the seventh working of the pattern
chart) and the back measures approximately 50 (52)cm from the cast-on edge.
Shape shoulders: Continuing in pattern,
cast off 13 (14) sts at the beginning of the
next 4 rows. Then cast off 12 sts at the
beginning of the following 2 rows. Cast off
the remaining sts across back of neck.

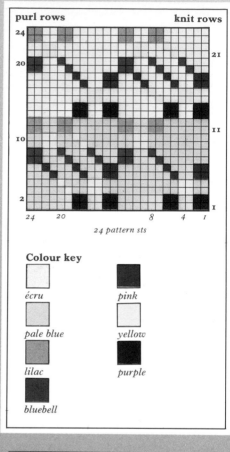

purl rows   **knit rows**

24 pattern sts

Colour key

écru   pink

pale blue   yellow

lilac   purple

bluebell

FRONTS

Pocket linings
Begin by making the pocket linings as
follows: with 2¾mm needles and yarn A,
cast on 28 (32) sts. Work 6cm in st st in
yarn A, ending with a knit row. Leave the
sts on a spare needle and make another
lining in the same way.

Left front
With 2¾mm needles and yarn A, cast on
58 (62) sts. Work 5cm in k1, p1 twisted rib
in yarn A, increasing across the last
wrong-side row as follows: rib 5 (1) sts,
*rib 2 sts, rib twice into the next st, rib 2
(3) sts; repeat from * nine more times, rib
3 (1) sts – 68 (72) sts.
Change to 3¼mm needles and st st and
work pattern from chart, reading knit rows
from right to left and purl rows from left
to right. Work the pattern across knit rows
as follows: *for the smaller size (86cm)*,
work sts *1–24* twice then work sts *1–20* to
finish the row; *for the larger size (91cm)*,
work sts *1–24* three times across the row.
Work purl rows in reverse. Continue thus
in pattern until you have worked row 12 of
the chart.

Pocket: Introduce the pocket in row 13
as follows: continuing in pattern, work the
first 20 sts of the row, cast off the next 28
(32) sts and then work the pattern across
the remaining 20 sts in the row. On the
next row, work the pattern across the first
20 sts, then continue in pattern across the
28 (32) sts of one pocket lining on spare
needle, and then work the pattern to the
end of the row.
Continuing in pattern, work straight until
you have completed row 12 (16) of the
fourth working of the pattern chart, and
front measures the same as the back from
cast-on edge to start of armhole shaping –
approximately 31 (32)cm.

continued on p. 73

MATERIALS Jacket

Yarn
Use 2-ply jumper weight Shetland yarn
unless otherwise indicated.
Yarn A 100g *(wine)*
Yarn B 75g *(olive)*
Yarn C 75g lurex *(mustard)*
Yarn D 100g *(copper)*
Yarn E 75g *(pale lilac mix)*
Yarn F 75g *(fawn)*
Yarn G 75g *(peat)*
Yarn H 75g *(chocolate)*
Yarn K 75g *(dark wine mix)*

Needles
1 pair size 3¼mm
1 pair size 2¾mm
1 crochet hook, size 2¾mm

Notions
1 button

MEASUREMENTS
To fit chest 86 (91, 97)cm (34, 36, 38in).
(See also chart on p. 120.)

Tension
31 sts and 32 rows measure 10cm over
Fair Isle pattern on 3¼mm needles.

continued on p. 72

STERLING ZIG-ZAG

*Subtle shades of Shetland yarn, enhanced with specks of copper
make this peplum skirted jacket an ideal garment for winter evenings.
The one-size camisole top is worked entirely in striped rib
following the same colours as the rib in the jacket.*

MATERIALS Camisole

Yarn

Use 2-ply jumper weight Shetland yarn
unless otherwise indicated.
Yarn A 50g *(peat)*
Yarn B 50g *(wine)*
Yarn C 50g lurex *(copper)*
Needles
1 pair size 3mm

MEASUREMENTS

One-size: to fit bust 86cm (34in).
(See also chart on p. 120.)
Tension
36 sts and 36 rows measure 10cm over
pattern on 3mm needles.

BACK

**With 3mm needles and yarn B, cast on
120 sts. Work the entire back in k1, p1
twisted rib in the following three-colour
stripe sequence:
Row 1: Yarn A
Row 2: Yarn C
Row 3: Yarn B
Continue repeating rows 1–3 up the back,
carrying yarn not in use up the sides of
the work, until back measures 29cm from
cast-on edge**. Cast off in rib in yarn B.

FRONT

Work as for back from ** to **. Then
divide for the shaped top as follows: on
the next (right-side) row, rib the first 60
sts of row and then turn, leaving the
remaining 60 sts on a spare needle or
stitch holder. Continue in rib on these
first 60 sts, decreasing one st at each end
of the next and every following alternate
row, 27 times in all – 6 sts remain.
Continuing in striped rib on these 6 sts,
work 36cm to form shoulder strap. Cast
off. Shape the remaining 60 sts on spare
needle in the same way, continuing on
into strap as before. Cast off.

TO MAKE UP

Darn in any loose ends at the sides. Join
side seams. Measure a point 8cm in from
each side seam and mark with a pin. Pin
shoulder straps in position at each pin
point, adjust if necessary and then sew in
position. Do not press the camisole.

STIRLING ZIG-ZAG

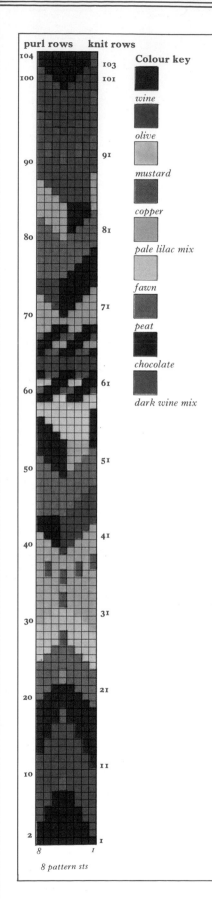

purl rows   knit rows

104   103

Colour key

wine

olive

mustard

copper

pale lilac mix

fawn

peat

chocolate

dark wine mix

8 pattern sts

BACK

With 2¾mm needles and yarn K, cast on 272 (288, 304) sts. Work 9 rows in k1, p1 twisted rib in the following three-colour sequence, starting with a wrong-side row:

Rows 1, 4, 7: Yarn G
Rows 2, 5, 8: Yarn D
Rows 3, 6, 9: Yarn A

Carry yarns not in use up the sides of the work. Change to 3¼mm needles and st st and work Fair Isle pattern from chart, reading odd (knit) rows from right to left and even (purl) rows from left to right. Repeat the 8 pattern sts 34 (36, 38) times across the rows. Continue in pattern until you have worked row 54 (58, 62) of the chart. With right side facing, decrease for waist as follows: k2 tog right across row – 136 (144, 152) sts.

Waistband: Change to 2¾mm needles and work rows 1–9 of striped rib as before. Then work rows 1–2 again. Change to 3¼mm needles and st st and continue in Fair Isle pattern from row 55 (59, 63) of the first working of the chart until you have completed row 14 (22, 30) of the second working of the chart and the back measures approximately 20 (22, 24)cm from the top of the waistband.

Shape armholes: Continuing in pattern, cast off 8 sts at the beginning of the next 2 rows. Then decrease one st at each end of every row until 102 (110, 118) sts remain. Work straight in pattern until you have worked row 76 (88, 100) of the second working of the pattern chart and the armhole measures approximately 19 (20, 22)cm from start of armhole shaping.

Shape shoulders: Continuing in pattern, cast off 8 sts at the beginning of the next 4 rows. Then cast off 5 (6, 7) sts at the beginning of the following 6 rows. Leave the remaining 40 (42, 44) sts on a spare needle or stitch holder.

FRONTS

Left front

With 2¾mm needles and yarn A, cast on 124 (132, 140) sts. Work rows 1–9 of striped rib as before.

Change to 3¼mm needles and st st and work pattern from chart, repeating sts 1–8 15 (16, 17) times across and then working sts 1–4 to finish the rows. Continue in pattern until you have completed row 54 (58, 62) of the chart. On the next row, decrease for waist as follows: k2 tog right across row – 62 (66, 70) sts.

Waistband: Change to 2¾mm needles and work rows 1–9 of striped rib as before, starting on a wrong-side row. Then work rows 1–2 of rib again. Change to 3¼mm needles and st st and continue in pattern from row 55 (59, 63) of the first working of the chart until you have worked row 14 (22, 30) of the second working of the chart and front measures approximately 20 (22, 24)cm from the top of the waistband.

Shape armhole: Continuing in pattern, cast off 8 sts at the beginning of the next (right-side) row. Then decrease one st at

the armhole edge on every row until 45 (49, 53) sts remain. Then work straight in pattern for the next 32 (36, 40) rows, ending at the neck edge.

Shape neck: Continuing in pattern, cast off 3 sts at the beginning of the next (wrong-side) row. Then k2 tog at the neck edge on every row until 31 (34, 38) sts remain. Work straight in pattern until you have worked row 76 (88, 100) of the second working of the pattern chart and armhole measures approximately 19 (20, 22)cm from start of armhole shaping.

Shape shoulder: Continuing in pattern, cast off 8 sts at the beginning of the next and following alternate row three times. Work one row straight. Then cast off 7 (5, 7) sts at the beginning of the next row. *For the two larger sizes,* work one row purl, then cast off the remaining 5 (7) sts.

Right front

Work as for left front but reverse all shapings.

SLEEVES

With 2¾mm needles and yarn A, cast on 62 (62, 64) sts. Work 24 rows in striped rib as before, repeating rows 1–3 eight times, then work rows 1 and 2 again. Increase across the next (wrong-side) row as follows: (yarn A) purl 10 (10, 8) sts, *make one st, rib one st; repeat from * to last 11 (11, 9) sts, make one st, purl to end of row – 104 (104, 112) sts.

Change to 3¼mm needles and st st and work Fair Isle pattern from chart, beginning at row 3 (7, 11) of chart. Continue in pattern until you have worked row 14 (22, 30) of the second working of the pattern chart and the sleeve measures approximately 43 (44, 45)cm from the cast-on edge.

Shape top of sleeve: Cast off 8 sts at the beginning of the next 2 rows. Then k2 tog at each end of the next and every following alternate row 7 (10, 10) times. Work 13 (17, 16) rows straight. K2 tog at each end of the next and every following row, 10 (8, 6) times. Purl one row. Cast off remaining sts. Repeat for other sleeve.

FRONT BANDS

Begin by joining the fronts to the back at shoulders.

Left front

With 2¾mm needles and yarn A, and with right side facing, pick up and knit 171 (181, 191) sts down left front opening edge, from start of neck shaping to bottom edge of ribbing. Work rows 1–9 of striped rib as before. Cast off in rib in yarn A.

Right front

Beginning at bottom edge pick up and knit 171 (181, 191) sts as far as start of neck shaping. Work to correspond with left front band.

NECKBAND

With right side facing, using 2¾mm needles and yarn A, starting at inner (picked-up) edge of right front band, pick up and knit 97 (99, 101) sts around neck edge as far as inner edge of left front band, including the sts on spare needle at back of neck. Work rows 1–9 of striped rib as before. Then cast off in rib in yarn A.

TO MAKE UP

Press all pieces lightly from wrong side, avoiding ribbing. Join both side seams and sleeve seams. Sew in sleeves, gathering fullness around top of sleeve, to fit armhole. Crochet a chain loop for button and sew to left front band at waistband. Sew on button to right front band to match. Press all seams.

Shape armhole: Continuing in pattern, cast off 10 (13) sts at the beginning of the next row. Then work armhole edge straight until you have worked row 21 of the fifth working of the pattern chart (row 7 of the sixth working of the chart) and armhole measures 11 (12)cm from the start of armhole shaping.

Shape neck: Continuing in pattern, cast off 4 sts at the beginning of the next (wrong-side) row, then decrease one st at the neck edge on the following 16 (15) rows – 38 (40) sts remain. Then work straight in pattern until you have completed row 24 of the sixth working of the pattern chart (row 8 of the seventh working of the pattern chart) and the front measures the same as the back from cast-on edge to start of shoulder shaping – approximately 50 (52)cm.

Shape shoulder: Continuing in pattern, cast off 13 (14) sts at the beginning of the next and the following alternate row. Work one row straight and then cast off 12 sts at the beginning of the next row.

Right front

Work as for left front, but reverse pocket, armhole, neck and shoulder shapings.

SLEEVES

With 2¾mm needles and yarn A, cast on 56 (60) sts. Work 11cm in k1, p1 twisted rib increasing across the last (wrong-side) row as follows: rib 8 (10) sts, *rib one st, rib twice into the next st; repeat from * 19 more times, rib 8 (10) sts – 76 (80) sts. Change to 3¼mm needles and st st and work pattern from chart, beginning with row 13 (1) of the chart. *For the smaller size* (86cm), starting at row 13 so that pattern matches at armhole, repeat sts 1–24 three times across the row and then work sts 1–4 (inclusive) to finish the row; *for the larger size* (91cm), repeat sts 1–24 three times across the row and then work sts 1–8 once to finish the row. Work purl rows in reverse. Continuing in pattern shape side edges by increasing one st at each end of the 15th (3rd) row and every following fourth row until there are 130 (136) sts on the needle, taking the extra sts into the pattern as they are made. Then work straight in pattern until you have completed row 12 (24) of the sixth (fifth) working of the pattern chart. (It is the sixth working of the pattern chart for the smaller size because you have worked rows 15–24 of the first pattern, then 4 complete patterns, then rows 1–12 of the sixth.) Cast off right across row; this cast-off edge should measure 41 (43)cm to fit armhole.

Make another sleeve in the same way.

FRONT BANDS

Right front

With 2¾mm needles and yarn A, and with right side of work facing, beginning at lower edge, pick up and knit 141 (148) sts up right front opening edge to start of neck shaping. Work 5 rows in twisted rib in yarn A.

Buttonholes: Make 8 buttonholes in the next row as follows: rib 3 sts, *cast off 3 sts, rib 16 (17) sts; repeat from * six more times, cast off 3 sts, rib 2 sts. Rib back along the next row, casting on 3 sts directly over those cast off in the previous row. Work 4 more rows of twisted rib in yarn A. Cast off in rib.

Left front

Work as for right front but begin at start of neck shaping and omit buttonholes.

COLLAR

With 2¾mm needles and yarn A, cast on 109 (113) sts. Work one row in twisted rib in yarn A. Continuing in rib in yarn A, increase one st at each end of the next and following 5 alternate rows. Then increase one st at each end of the next 6 rows – 133 (137) sts. Work 4 (6) rows straight in rib. Then decrease one st at each end of the next 6 rows, then decrease one st at each of the following 6 alternate rows – 109 (113) sts. Work a further row in rib in yarn A; then cast off in rib.

POCKETS

Pocket tops

With right side of work facing, using 2¾mm needles and yarn A, pick up and knit 28 (32) sts along lower cast-off edge of one pocket slit. Work 8 rows in twisted rib in yarn A, then cast off in rib. Repeat for other pocket.

TO MAKE UP

Press all pieces lightly from wrong side, avoiding ribbing. Join side and shoulder seams. Join each sleeve seam, leaving 4 (5)cm unstitched at the top of the seam. Pin straight edge around top of sleeve into top of armhole, and pin each side of the unstitched sleeve seam across the straight cast-off edge at the bottom of the armhole. Sew in place and repeat for other sleeve. With right side facing, pin cast-on, shaped edge of collar around neck edge, beginning and ending at start of front bands. Sew in position. Fold the collar in half so that cast-off, shaped edge just covers the first seam. Pin and sew in position. Sew down sides of pocket tops and sew around each pocket lining on wrong side. Sew on 8 buttons to left front band to match buttonholes. Cut elastic to fit around bottom of cardigan and thread through cast-on edge of welt from wrong side; secure ends of elastic.

CHITIMACHA

A men's or women's waistcoat with a double thickness shawl collar.
A section of the pattern is used to border the pockets and armholes
and the front edges are self-faced.

MATERIALS

Yarn
Use 2-ply jumper weight Shetland yarn.
Different sizes require different quantities
of yarn.
Yarn A 125 (175)g *(rust)*
Yarn B 50 (75)g *(mustard)*
Yarn C 50 (75)g *(jade mix)*
Yarn D 50g *(oat)*
Yarn E 100 (125)g *(black)*

Needles
1 pair size 3¼mm
1 pair size 3mm
1 pair size 2¾mm

Notions
5 buttons (leather)

MEASUREMENTS

To fit chest 86–91 (102–106)cm (34–36,
40–42in).
(See also chart on p. 120.)

Tension
30 sts and 32 rows measure 10cm over
Fair Isle pattern on 3¼mm needles.

BACK

With 2¾mm needles and yarn E, cast on
120 (130) sts. Work 4cm in k1, p1 twisted
rib in yarn E, increasing 10 sts across the
last (wrong-side) row *for the larger size
only*, by working twice into every 13th st –
120 (140) sts.

Change to 3¼mm needles and st st and
work Fair Isle pattern from chart, reading
odd (knit) rows from right to left and even
(purl) rows from left to right. Work the
pattern across knit rows as follows: *for the
smaller size*, repeat sts *1–40* three times;
for the larger size, repeat sts *1–40* three
times and then work sts *1–20* once to
complete row. Work purl rows in reverse.
At the same time, shape the sides by
increasing one st at each end of the 5th
and every following 4th row until there
are 140 (160) sts on the needle, taking the
extra sts into the pattern as they are made.
Work straight in pattern until you have
worked row 14 (30) of the second working
of the chart and back measures approximately 26 (31)cm from cast-on edge.
Shape armholes: Continuing in pattern,
cast off 16 sts at the beginning of the next
2 rows. Then decrease one st at each end
of the next 3 rows – 102 (122) sts. Now
work straight until you have completed
row 18 (46) of the third working of chart
and back measures approximately 23
(27)cm from start of armhole shaping.
Shape shoulders: Cast off 6 (8) sts at the
beginning of the next 6 rows; then cast off
6 sts at the beginning of the following 2
rows – 54 (62) sts remain.
Shape collar: Work 12 rows straight in
pattern on these 54 (62) sts. Increase one
st at each end of next and every following
alternate row until there are 74 (82) sts on
the needle – 19 rows. Decrease one st at
each end of every following alternate row
until 56 (64) sts remain – 18 rows.
Decrease one st at each end of next row.
Work 12 rows straight. Cast off.

FRONTS

Right front
With 2¾mm needles and yarn E, cast on
80 (90) sts. Work 4 rows in k1, p1 twisted
rib in yarn E.
Buttonholes: Work the first buttonhole as

follows: on the next (right-side) row rib 6
sts, cast off 4 sts, rib 12 sts and cast off 4
sts; rib to end of row. On the next row,
rib to the last 25 sts, cast on 4 sts directly
over those cast off in previous row, rib 12
sts, cast on 4 sts and rib to end of row.
Continue in k1, p1 twisted rib in yarn E
until welt measures 4cm from cast-on edge.
Change to 3¼mm needles and st st and
work Fair Isle pattern from chart. Work
the pattern across knit rows as follows:
for the smaller size, work sts *1–40* twice;
for the larger size, work sts *1–40* twice and
then work sts *1–10* once to complete row.
   Work purl rows in reverse. Increase one

st at the side seam edge on the 5th and every following 4th row, ten times in all, until there are 90 (100) sts on the needle, taking the extra sts into the pattern as they are made. *At the same time*, on row 15 (19) of the first working of the pattern chart, work the second buttonhole and the pocket opening as follows: continuing in pattern, work the first 6 sts of the row, then cast off 4 sts, work the next 10 sts, cast off 4 sts and then work pattern to the last 20 (26) sts in row. Turn and work back across next 32 sts in purl in yarn A. Turn again, join in yarn C, and work pocket lining on these 32 sts. Work 13cm in st st in yarn C, ending with a knit row, so forming pocket lining. Now continue in pattern across the last 20 (26) sts of row 15 (19) from where you broke off to work pocket lining. To finish buttonhole, on the next row – row 16 (20) – work back along row in pattern until beginning of first cast-off buttonhole edge (last 24 sts in row). Cast on 4 sts directly over those cast off in row 15 (19), work the next 10 sts in pattern, cast on 4 sts over the next cast-off edge and then work the remaining 6 sts of row. Continuing in pattern, increase one st at the side edge on every 4th row until there are 90 (100) sts on needle. *At the same time*, make a buttonhole every 20 (24) rows, i.e. make third buttonhole on row 35 (43) of first working of the pattern chart, 4th buttonhole on row 55 (5) of first (second) working of chart, 5th buttonhole on row 13 (29) of the fifth working of chart. Work each buttonhole in the same way as row 15 (19), taking into account extra sts at side edge. *Meanwhile*, when there are 90 (100) sts on needle, work straight until you have completed row 13 (29) of the second working of chart and front measures approximately 26 (31)cm from cast-on edge.

Shape armhole: Continuing in pattern, at the beginning of the next (wrong-side) row, cast off 16 sts and then work to end of row. Then decrease one st at the armhole edge on the next 3 rows – 71 (81) sts. Then work armhole edge straight.

Shape collar: Continuing in pattern, increase one st at the front edge on the next row – row 18 (34) of second working of pattern chart – and every following alternate row until there are 79 (89) sts on the needle. Then work straight until front measures approximately 23 (27)cm, ending with a knit row, i.e. row 17 (45) of third working of chart.

Shape shoulder: Cast off 6 (8) sts at the beginning of the next and the following 2 alternate rows; then cast off 6 sts at the beginning of the following alternate row – 55 (59) sts. Cast off remaining sts.

Left front
Work as for right front but omit buttonholes and reverse pocket, armhole, collar

and shoulder shapings. When starting pocket lining on row 15 (19) work as follows: work the first 52 (58) sts of row in pattern; turn, purl back across the 32 sts of next row in yarn A; turn, join in yarn C and work 13cm in st st, then complete pattern across remaining sts in row 15 (19) as before.

ARMHOLE BANDS

Join fronts to back at shoulders. With 3mm needles and yarn E, pick up 160 (180) sts around armhole. Work one row purl in yarn E. Turn back to chart. Work the pattern across knit rows as follows: *for the smaller size*, repeat sts 1–40 four times; *for the larger size*, repeat sts 1–40 four times, then work sts 1–20 once. Work rows 1–5 of chart. Change to yarn E and work a further row in purl in yarn E. Change to 2¾mm needles, work 9 rows in k1, p1 twisted rib in yarn E, to form facing. Cast off.

TO MAKE UP

Using a bodkin or blunt needle, darn in any loose ends of yarn. Press all pieces lightly from the wrong side avoiding

ribbing. Sew side seams.
Armhole bands: Join bands at underarm points with a flat seam. Fold bands in half so that ribbing just shows at edge of armhole and pin and sew inner cast-off edge of ribbing in position around inside of armhole. Repeat for other armhole.
Front facings and buttonholes: Fold right front facing edge to inside so that buttonhole edges align and pin. Then sew this inner edge in position and oversew around the double cast-off edges of each buttonhole. Sew inner edge of left front facing in position, turning in the same amount of facing as for right front facing. Sew edges of back collar to top edge of shawl collar on right and left fronts with flat seams. Then fold entire collar over and pin and slip stitch inner edge in position inside. Oversew the sides of each pocket lining together, leaving linings free from main work. Sew on buttons to match buttonholes. Press.

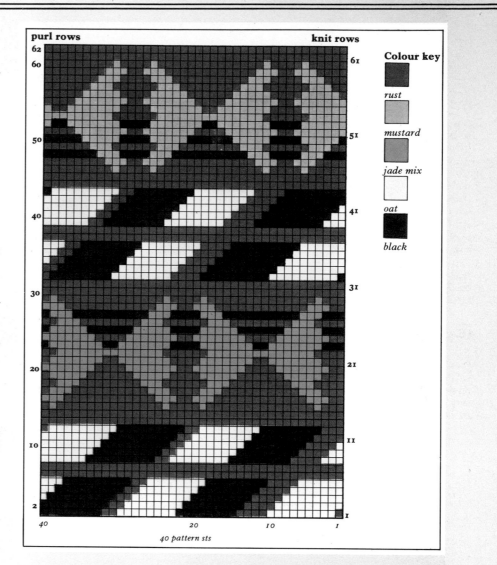

purl rows / knit rows

Colour key

rust

mustard

jade mix

oat

black

40 pattern sts

WILLOW

Chinese willow pattern in blue and white makes an ingenious design for this simple waistcoat. The back is worked in plain rib and the ribbed bands are edged with navy yarn.

MATERIALS

Yarn
Use 2-ply jumper weight Shetland yarn.
Yarn A 150g *(mid-blue mix)*
Yarn B 75g *(ivory)*
Yarn C 25g *(navy)*

Needles
1 pair size 3¼mm
1 pair size 2¾mm

Notions
5 buttons

MEASUREMENTS

To fit chest 91 (97)cm (36, 38in).
(See also chart on p. 120.)

Tension
32 sts and 32 rows measure 10cm over Willow pattern on 3¼mm needles.

FRONTS

Left front
With 2¾mm needles and yarn A, cast on 72 (77) sts. Work 5cm in k1, p1 twisted rib in yarn A.
Change to 3¼mm needles and work Willow pattern from chart, reading odd (knit) rows from right to left and even (purl) rows from left to right. *For the smaller size,* work sts *1–72* once and *for the larger size,* work sts *1–77* once across knit rows. Work purl rows in reverse. Continue to work straight in pattern until you have completed row 76 (80) of the pattern chart and the front measures approximately 29 (30)cm from the cast-on edge.
Shape armhole and neck: Continuing in pattern, cast off 10 (12) sts at the beginning of the next row; then work pattern across to the last 2 sts, k2 tog. Now decrease one st at the armhole edge on the next 21 rows and then work the armhole edge straight. *At the same time,* continue to decrease one st at the neck edge on every following 4th row after the first decrease on row 77 (81) until 27 (30) sts remain. Then work straight in pattern until you have completed row 62 (70) of the second working of the pattern chart and the front measures approximately 51 (53)cm from the cast-on edge.
Shape shoulder: Continuing in pattern, cast off 9 (10) sts at the beginning of the next and following 2 alternate rows.

Right front
Work the same as left front, reversing armhole, neck and shoulder shapings.

BACK

With 2¾mm needles and yarn A, cast on 148 (156) sts. Work 5cm in k1, p1 twisted rib in yarn A.
Change to 3¼mm needles and continue to work entire back in rib in A. Work straight until back measures 29 (30)cm and matches front from cast-on edge to start of armhole shaping, ending on a wrong-side row.
Shape armholes: Cast off 6 sts at beginning of next 2 rows. K2 tog each end of every row until 100 (108) sts remain. Work straight until back matches fronts from cast-on edge to start of shoulder shaping.
Shape shoulders: Cast off 9 (10) sts at beginning of next 6 rows. Divide remaining 46 (48) sts in half. Leave each half on a spare needle or stitch holder.

Join fronts to back at shoulders.

purl rows — knit rows

77 pattern sts

Colour key
mid-blue mix
ivory

FRONT BANDS

Right front

With right side of work facing, using 2¾mm needles and yarn A, beginning at the hem edge, pick up and knit 93 (97) sts up right front opening edge as far as start of neck shaping; then pick up and knit a further 100 (104) sts around neck to centre-back, including the 23 (24) sts on the first spare needle. Work 3 rows in k1, p1 twisted rib.

Buttonholes: Make five buttonholes in the 4th row of ribbing as follows: rib 4 sts, *cast off 3 sts, rib 18 (19) sts; repeat from * three more times, cast off 3 sts, rib to end of row. Rib back along the 5th row of ribbing, casting on 3 sts directly over those cast off in the previous row. Work 4 more rows in rib in yarn A. Join in yarn C and work one more row in rib in yarn C. Cast off in rib in yarn C.

Left front

Work in the same way as for right front band, but begin at the centre-back of neck with the remaining 23 (24) sts on spare needle and then pick up and knit 170 (177) sts to hem edge, and omit the buttonholes.

ARMBANDS

With right side of work facing, using 2¾mm needles and yarn A, pick up and knit 152 (160) sts around one armhole. Work 9 rows in twisted rib in yarn A. Join in yarn C and work a further row of rib in yarn C. Cast off in rib in yarn C. Repeat for other armhole.

TO MAKE UP

Press fronts lightly from the wrong side, avoiding ribbing. Join fronts to back at side seams. Join ribbing at back of neck. Sew on buttons to left front band to correspond with buttonholes. Press seams lightly from wrong side.

ISLAMIC

*A patterned waistcoat with front pockets and striped rib back.
The pattern comes from old Islamic geometric designs
and is bordered here with chocolate brown and wine.*

MATERIALS

Yarn
Use 2-ply jumper weight Shetland yarn.
Different sizes will require different
quantities of main yarn.
Yarn A 75 (75, 100)g *(chocolate)*
Yarn B 50g *(peat)*
Yarn C 50g *(wine)*
Yarn D 25g *(powder blue)*
Yarn E 25g *(ivory)*
Yarn F 25g *(orange mix)*
Yarn G 25g *(blue/orange mix)*
Yarn H 25g *(lilac/green mix)*
Yarn J 25g *(royal blue)*

Needles
1 pair size 3¼mm
1 pair size 3mm
1 pair size 2¾mm

Notions
5 buttons

MEASUREMENTS

To fit chest 84 (91, 99)cm (33, 36, 39in).
(See also chart on p. 120.)

Tension
32 sts and 32 rows measure 10cm over
Fair Isle pattern on 3¼mm needles.

FRONTS

Pocket linings
Begin by making the pocket linings. With
3mm needles and yarn A, cast on 28 (32,
36) sts and work 7cm in st st, ending with
a purl row. Transfer the sts to a spare
needle or stitch holder. Make another
pocket lining in the same way.

Left front
**With 2¾mm needles and yarn A cast on
66 (72, 78) sts. Work 5cm in k1, p1
twisted rib in yarn A**.
Change to 3¼mm needles and st st and
work Fair Isle pattern from chart, reading
odd (knit) rows from right to left and even
(purl) rows from left to right. Work the
pattern across knit rows as follows: *for the
small size (84cm)*, repeat sts *1–16* four
times across row and then work sts *1–2*
once; *for the medium size (91cm)*, repeat
sts *1–16* four times and then work sts *1–8*
once; *for the large size (99cm)*, repeat sts
1–16 four times and then work sts *1–14*
once. Work purl rows in reverse. Continue
in pattern until you have worked row 14
of the chart.

Pocket: Introduce pocket in row 15 as
follows: knit the first 19 (20, 21) sts of the
row, then transfer the next 28 (32, 36) sts
to a spare needle or stitch holder, and in
their place take into the pattern the 28
(32, 36) sts of one pocket lining on spare
needle; then work the remaining 19 (20,
21) sts of the row in pattern. Continuing
in pattern work straight until you have

worked row 28 (32, 36) of the second
working of the pattern chart and the front
measures approximately 29 (30, 32)cm
from the cast-on edge.

Shape armhole and neck edge: At the
beginning of the next row, cast off 8 (10,
12) sts, then work in pattern to the last 2
sts; k2 tog. Continuing in pattern, decrease one st at the armhole edge on the
next 14 (16, 18) rows; then work armhole
edge straight. *At the same time*, continue
to decrease one st at the neck edge on
every following 4th row after the first
decrease on row 29 (33, 37), 8 (9, 13)
times. Then decrease one st on every
following 3rd row until 24 (26, 28) sts
remain. Work straight in pattern until you
have worked row 50 (6, 12) of the third
(fourth, fourth) working of the chart and
armhole measures approximately 22 (23,
24)cm from start of armhole shaping.

Shape shoulder: Continuing in pattern,
cast off 8 (10, 10) sts at the beginning of
the next row, then 8 (8, 9) sts at the beginning of the following 2 alternate rows.

Right front
Work welt as for front from ** to **.
Change to 3¼mm needles and st st and
work Fair Isle pattern from chart as
before. Work as for left front, introducing
remaining pocket lining and reversing all
shapings.

BACK

With 2¾mm needles and yarn A, cast on
132 (144, 156) sts. Work 5cm k1, p1
twisted rib in yarn A.
Change to 3mm needles and continue to
work entire back in twisted rib, working
the following five-colour stripe sequence:

Row 1: Yarn B
Row 2: Yarn C
Row 3: Yarn H
Row 4: Yarn J
Row 5: Yarn A

Carry yarns not in use up the sides of the
work and continue repeating these rows
1–5 until the back measures the same as
the front from the cast-on edge to the
start of the armhole shaping – approximately 29 (30, 32)cm.

Shape armholes: Continuing in striped
rib, on the next right-side row, cast off
3 (4, 6) sts at the beginning of this and the
next row. Then k2 tog at each end of
every row until 100 (104, 108) sts remain.
Work straight until the back measures the
same as the front from beginning of armhole shaping to beginning of shoulder
shaping – approximately 22 (23, 24)cm.

Shape shoulders: Continuing in striped
rib, on the next right-side row, cast off 10
(11, 10) sts at the beginning of this and
the next row. Then cast off 9 (9, 10) sts at

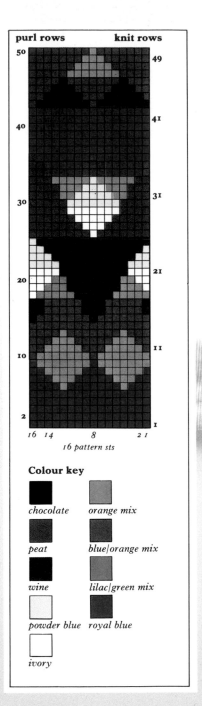

purl rows   knit rows

16 14   8   2 1

16 pattern sts

Colour key

■ *chocolate*	■ *orange mix*
■ *peat*	■ *blue/orange mix*
■ *wine*	■ *lilac/green mix*
□ *powder blue*	■ *royal blue*
□ *ivory*	

the beginning of the following 4 rows.
Divide the remaining 44 (46, 48) sts in
half and transfer each half to a spare
needle or stitch holder.

Join fronts to back at shoulders.

FRONT BANDS

Right front

With 2¾mm needles and yarn A, beginning at hem edge, pick up and knit 93 (97, 101) sts up the front opening edge as far as the start of the neck shaping. Then continue to pick up and knit 81 (87, 93) sts around the neck edge as far as the centre-back, including the 22 (23, 24) sts on the first spare needle – 174 (184, 194) sts in all. Work 3 rows of k1, p1 twisted rib in yarn A.

Buttonholes: Make five buttonholes in the 4th row or ribbing as follows: rib 4 sts, *cast off 3 sts, rib 18 (19, 20) sts; repeat from * 3 more times, cast off 3 sts and rib to end of row. On row 5 of ribbing, rib back, casting on 3 sts directly over each of the five cast-off stitches in the previous row. Then work 4 more rows in twisted rib in yarn A. Join in yarn C and work one row of twisted rib in yarn C. Cast off in rib in yarn C.

Left front

With 2¾mm needles and yarn A, beginning at the centre-back of the neck, rib the 22 (23, 24) sts on the remaining needle, then pick up and knit 59 (64, 69) sts around neck to start of neck shaping and a further 93 (97, 101) sts down front opening edge to hem edge – 174 (184, 194) sts in all. Work 9 rows of twisted rib in yarn A. Join in yarn C, work one row of twisted rib and then cast off in rib in yarn C.

ARMHOLE BANDS

With 2¾mm needles and yarn A, and with right side facing, pick up and knit 144 (150, 156) sts around one armhole. Work 9 rows of twisted rib in yarn A. Change to yarn C and work one row of rib in yarn C. Cast off in rib in yarn C. Repeat for other armhole.

POCKETS

Pocket tops

With 2¾mm needles and yarn A, knit across the 28 (32, 36) sts of one pocket opening on spare needle. Then work 9 rows of twisted rib in yarn A. Change to yarn C and work a further row in twisted rib in yarn C. Cast off in rib in yarn C. Repeat for other pocket top.

TO MAKE UP

Press fronts lightly from wrong side, avoiding ribbing. Sew ribbed borders together at centre-back of neck. Join fronts to back at sides. Sew pocket linings to wrong side of waistcoat fronts. Sew down sides of pocket tops. Sew 5 buttons to left front band to correspond with buttonholes. Press seams lightly from wrong side.

back of waistcoat

LEAVES

A warm winter cardigan based on a Fair Isle pattern,
inspired by autumn leaves and colours.

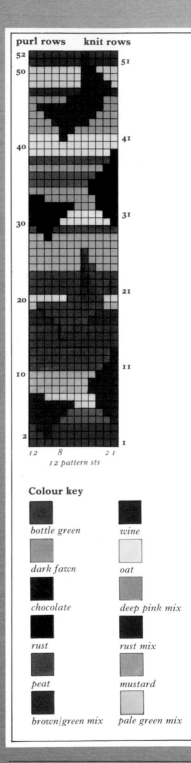

purl rows   knit rows

52   51
50
40   41
30   31
20   21
10   11
2   1

12   8   2 1
12 pattern sts

Colour key

bottle green   wine

dark fawn   oat

chocolate   deep pink mix

rust   rust mix

peat   mustard

brown/green mix   pale green mix

MATERIALS

Yarn
Use 2-ply jumper weight Shetland yarn.
Yarn A 100g *(bottle green)*
Yarn B 50g *(dark fawn)*
Yarn C 50g *(chocolate)*
Yarn D 50g *(rust)*
Yarn E 50g *(peat)*

Yarn F 50g *(brown/green mix)*
Yarn G 50g *(wine)*
Yarn H 50g *(oat)*
Yarn J 25g *(deep pink mix)*
Yarn K 25g *(rust mix)*
Yarn L 25g *(mustard)*
Yarn M 25g *(pale green mix)*

Needles
1 pair size 3¼mm
1 pair size 3mm
1 pair size 2¾mm

Notions
8 buttons

BACK

With 2¾mm needles and yarn A, cast on
123 (135) sts. Work 5 (6)cm in k1, p1
twisted rib, increasing across the last
(wrong-side) row as follows: rib 2 (8) sts,
*rib 6 sts, rib twice into the next st;
repeat from * 16 more times, rib 2 (8) sts –
140 (152) sts.
Change to 3¼mm needles and st st and
work Fair Isle pattern from chart, reading
odd (knit) rows from right to left and even
(purl) rows from left to right. Work the
pattern across knit rows as follows: *for the
smaller size* (86cm), repeat sts 1–12 eleven
times across the row and then work sts
1–8 once to complete row; *for the larger
size* (97cm), repeat sts 1–12 twelve times
across the row and then work sts 1–8 once
to complete row. Work purl rows in
reverse. Continuing thus in pattern work
straight until you have completed row 40
of the second working of the pattern chart
and the back measures approximately 34
(35)cm from the cast-on edge.
Shape armholes: Continuing in pattern,
cast off 10 (12) sts at the beginning of the
next 2 rows – 120 (128) sts remain. Now
work straight until you have worked row
52 of the third working of the pattern
chart (row 4 of the fourth working of the
pattern chart) and the back measures
approximately 53 (56)cm from the cast-
on edge.
Shape shoulders: Continuing in pattern,
cast off 13 (14) sts at the beginning of the
next 4 rows. Then cast off 11 (12) sts at
the beginning of the following 2 rows.
Cast off the remaining 46 (48) sts.

FRONTS

Pocket linings
Begin by making both pocket linings as
follows: with 3mm needles and yarn A,
cast on 26 (28) sts. Work 6cm in st st,
ending with a purl row.

Left front
With 2¾mm needles and yarn A, cast on
60 (64) sts. Work 5cm in k1, p1 twisted
rib, increasing across the last (wrong-side)
row as follows: rib 29 (30) sts, rib twice

into each of the next 2 (4) sts, rib 29 (30)
sts – 62 (68) sts.
Change to 3¼mm needles and st st and
work Fair Isle pattern from chart. Work
the pattern across knit rows as follows:
for the smaller size, repeat sts 1–12 five
times across and then work sts 1–2 once;
for the larger size, work sts 1–12 five times
across and then work sts 1–8 once. Work
purl rows in reverse. Continue thus in
pattern until you have worked row 13 of
the chart.
Pocket: Introduce the pocket in row 14
as follows: work the first 18 (20) sts in
row, cast off the next 26 (28) sts and then
work the pattern to end of row. Work the
pattern back across the first 18 (20) sts of
the next row (row 15), then continue to
work pattern across the 26 (28) sts of one
pocket lining on spare needle, work
pattern to end of row. Continuing in
pattern, work straight until you have
worked row 40 of the second working of
the pattern chart and the front measures
approximately 34 (35)cm from the cast-
on edge.
Shape armhole: Continuing in pattern,
cast off 10 (12) sts at the beginning of the
next row – 52 (56) sts. Now work straight
until you have completed row 27 (31) of
the third working of the pattern chart and
the front measures approximately 47
(49)cm from cast-on edge.
Shape neck: Continuing in pattern, cast
off 3 sts at the beginning of the next
(wrong-side) row. Then decrease one st at
the neck edge on the next 12 (13) rows –
37 (40) sts remain. Now work straight
until you have worked row 52 of the third
working of the chart (row 4 of the fourth
working of the chart) and the front
measures approximately 53 (56)cm from
cast-on edge.
Shape shoulder: Continuing in pattern,
cast off 13 (14) sts at the beginning of the
next and following alternate row. Work
one row straight, then cast off 11 (12) sts
at the beginning of the next row.

Right front
Work in the same way as left front, but
reverse pocket, armhole, neck and
shoulder shapings.

SLEEVES

With 2¾mm needles and yarn A, cast on
62 (64) sts. Work 10 (11)cm in k1, p1
twisted rib, increasing across the last
(wrong-side) row as follows: rib 4 (2) sts,
*rib twice into the next st, rib 2; repeat
from * 17 (19) more times, rib 4 (2) sts –
80 (84) sts.
Change to 3¼mm needles and st st and
work pattern from chart. Work the pattern
across knit rows as follows: *for the smaller
size,* repeat sts 1–12 six times and then

work sts *1–8* once to complete row; *for the larger size*, work sts *1–12* seven times. Continue thus in pattern, *at the same time*, shaping the sides by increasing one st at each end of the 3rd and every following 5th row until there are 128 (134) sts on the needle. Take the extra sts into the pattern as they are made. Then work straight in pattern until you have completed row 26 of third working of the chart and sleeve measures approximately 50 (51)cm. Cast off right across row; this cast-off edge should measure 41 (43)cm to fit armhole.

FRONT BANDS

Right front
With right side of work facing, using 2¾mm needles and yarn A, beginning at the lower edge, pick up and knit 149 (157) sts up right front opening edge to start of neck shaping. Work 5 rows in k1, p1 twisted rib.

Buttonholes: Make 8 buttonholes in the next row (row 6) as follows: rib 3 (4) sts, *cast off 3 sts, rib 17 (18) sts; repeat from * six more times, cast off 3 sts, rib 3 sts. Rib back along the next row (row 7), casting on 3 sts directly over those cast off in the previous row. Work a further 4 rows in rib. Cast off in rib.

Left front
In the same way, beginning at the start of the neck shaping, pick up and knit 149 (157) sts down left front opening edge to lower edge. Work band to correspond with right front band, but omit buttonholes.

COLLAR

With 2¾mm needles and yarn A cast on 115 sts. Work one row in k1, p1 twisted rib. Continuing in rib, increase one st at each end of the next and following 5 alternate rows – 127 sts. Now increase one st at each end of the next 6 rows 139 sts. Work 10cm straight in twisted rib. Then k2 tog at each end of the next 6 rows, then k2 tog at each end of the next and following 5 alternate rows – 115 sts. Work one row straight in rib; cast off in rib.

POCKETS

Pocket tops
With 2¾mm needles and yarn A, pick up and knit 26 (28) sts across the lower cast-off edge of one pocket. Work 10 rows in k1, p1 twisted rib; cast off in rib. Repeat for other pocket.

TO MAKE UP

Press all pieces from wrong side, avoiding all ribbing. Join shoulder seams. Join sleeve seams, leaving 4cm unstitched at top of seam. Pin top of sleeve into top of armhole and pin each side of unstitched section of sleeve seam across straight cast-off edge at bottom of armhole. Sew in position and repeat for other sleeve. With right side facing pin the cast-on and shaped edge of collar around neck edge, fitting it between the inner edges of the front bands. Sew in place and then fold collar in half so that the cast-off and

shaped edge just covers the seam. Pin this edge in position and sew neatly around neck. Sew the three sides of each pocket lining to the back of the cardigan fronts and catch down the sides of the pocket tops. Sew on 8 buttons to left front band to correspond with buttonholes. Press seams.

MEASUREMENTS

To fit chest 86 (91)cm (34, 36in).
(See also chart on p. 121.)

Tension
32 sts and 32 rows measure 10cm over Fair Isle pattern on 3¼mm needles.

MOSAIC

Based on the same geometric Islamic pattern as the waistcoat,
this gilet is ideal for both men and women.
The back is worked in striped rib.

MATERIALS

Yarn

Use 2-ply jumper weight Shetland yarn.
Different sizes will require different
quantities of yarn.
Yarn A 75 (75, 100)g *(navy)*
Yarn B 50 (50, 75)g *(rust)*
Yarn C 50 (50, 75)g *(olive)*
Yarn D 25 (25, 50)g *(bottle green)*
Yarn E 25g *(ivory)*
Yarn F 25g *(mustard mix)*
Yarn G 25g *(dark fawn)*
Yarn H 25g *(sage green)*
Yarn J 25g *(rust mix)*

Needles

1 pair size 3¼mm
1 pair size 3mm
1 pair size 2¼mm

MEASUREMENTS

To fit chest 91 (102, 112)cm (36, 40, 44in).
(See also chart on p. 121.)

Tension

31 sts and 30 rows measure 10cm over
Fair Isle pattern on 3¼mm needles.

back of waistcoat

FRONT

With 2¼mm needles and yarn A, cast on 130 (142, 152) sts. Work 5 (5, 6)cm in k1, p1 twisted rib in yarn A, increasing across the last wrong-side row as follows: rib one st, *rib 8 (6, 5) sts, rib twice into the next st; repeat from * 13 (19, 23) more times, rib 3 (1, 7) sts – 144 (160, 176) sts in all. Change to 3¼mm needles and st st and work Fair Isle pattern from chart, reading odd (knit) rows from right to left and even (purl) rows from left to right. Repeat the 16 pattern sts indicated on chart 9 (10, 11) times across the rows. Continuing in pattern work front straight until you have worked row 42 (46, 46) of the second working of the pattern chart and the front measures approximately 35 (37, 38)cm from the cast-on edge.

Shape armholes and neck: Continuing in pattern, cast off 11 (13, 15) sts at the beginning of the next 2 rows. K2 tog at beginning of next row, work next 59 (65, 71) sts of row in the pattern. Turn, leaving remaining sts in row on a spare needle. Work back across these 60 (66, 72) sts in pattern. *On the next row, k2 tog, then work pattern to end. Work the pattern across the next row. K2 tog at the beginning of the next row, work pattern to the last 2 sts, k2 tog. Work the pattern across the next row*. Continuing in pattern, repeat the 4 rows from * to * until 33 (35, 41) sts remain. Work armhole edge straight but continue to k2 tog at neck edge on every 4th row as before until 27 (30, 33) sts remain. Work straight until completing row 14 (22, 30) of fourth working of chart and front measures approx. 59 (62, 65)cm.
Shape shoulder: Cast off 9 (10, 11) sts at the beginning of the next and following 2 alternate rows.
Rejoin yarn to remaining sts on spare needle at neck edge and, continuing in pattern, shape right armhole and neck edge as follows: work the pattern across the next row to the last 2 sts, k2 tog. Work one row straight. **On the next row, work the pattern across to the last 2 sts, k2 tog. Work one row straight. K2 tog at the beginning of the next row, work pattern across to last 2 sts, k2 tog. Work one row straight.** Continuing in pattern, repeat these four rows from ** to **, until 33 (35, 41) sts remain. Finish to correspond with left shoulder, reversing all shapings.

BACK

With 2¼mm needles and yarn A, cast on 144 (160, 176) sts. Work 5 (5, 6)cm in k1, p1 twisted rib in yarn A. Change to 3mm needles and continue to work entire back in twisted rib in the following three-colour stripe sequence:
Row 1: Yarn B
Row 2: Yarn C
Row 3: Yarn A
Continue repeating rows 1–3 up the back, carrying yarns not in use up the sides of the work. Continue without shaping until back measures approximately 35 (37, 38)cm and matches the front from cast-on edge to start of armhole shaping, ending on a wrong-side row.
Shape armholes: Cast off 8 (10, 12) sts at the beginning of the next 2 rows. Then k2 tog at each end of every alternate row until 96 (106, 116) sts remain. Then work armhole edges straight until the back measures the same as the front from cast-on edge to start of shoulder shaping – approximately 59 (62, 55)cm – ending on a wrong-side row.
Shape shoulders: Cast off 9 (10, 11) sts at the beginning of the next 6 rows. Leave the remaining 42 (46, 50) sts on a spare needle.

NECKBAND

Join right shoulder seam.
With 2¼mm needles and yarn A, beginning at the left shoulder and with right side of work facing, pick up and knit 70 (74, 80) sts down left side of neck to centre of 'V'; mark this point with coloured thread. Then pick up and knit 2 sts from centre-front and mark again with coloured thread. Then pick up and knit 70 (74, 80) sts up right side of neck and the 42 (46, 50) sts on spare needle around back of neck – 184 (194, 210) sts. Work the neckband in k1, p1 twisted rib in yarn A, decreasing each side of the 2 centre-front sts as follows:
Row 1: Rib around back of neck and down right side of neck to within 2 sts of coloured thread, slip 1, k1, psso, p2, k2 tog, rib up left side of neck to end.
Row 2: Rib down left side of neck to within 2 sts of coloured thread, slip 1, k1, psso, k2, k2 tog, rib to end.
Repeat rows 1–2, four times, then work row 1 again. Join in yarn B and work one row in rib in yarn B as for row 2 above. Cast off in rib in yarn B.

ARMBANDS

Join left shoulder seam. With 2¼mm needles and yarn A, pick up and knit 172 (178, 186) sts around one armhole. Work 9 rows in twisted rib in yarn A. Join in yarn B and work a further row in rib in yarn B. Cast off in rib in yarn B. Repeat for other armhole.

TO MAKE UP

Join both side seams, joining ribbing at underarm points. Press lightly.

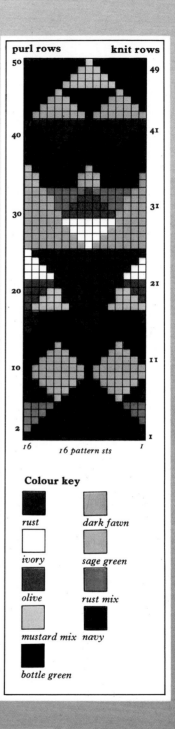

Colour key

rust

ivory

olive

mustard mix

bottle green

dark fawn

sage green

rust mix

navy

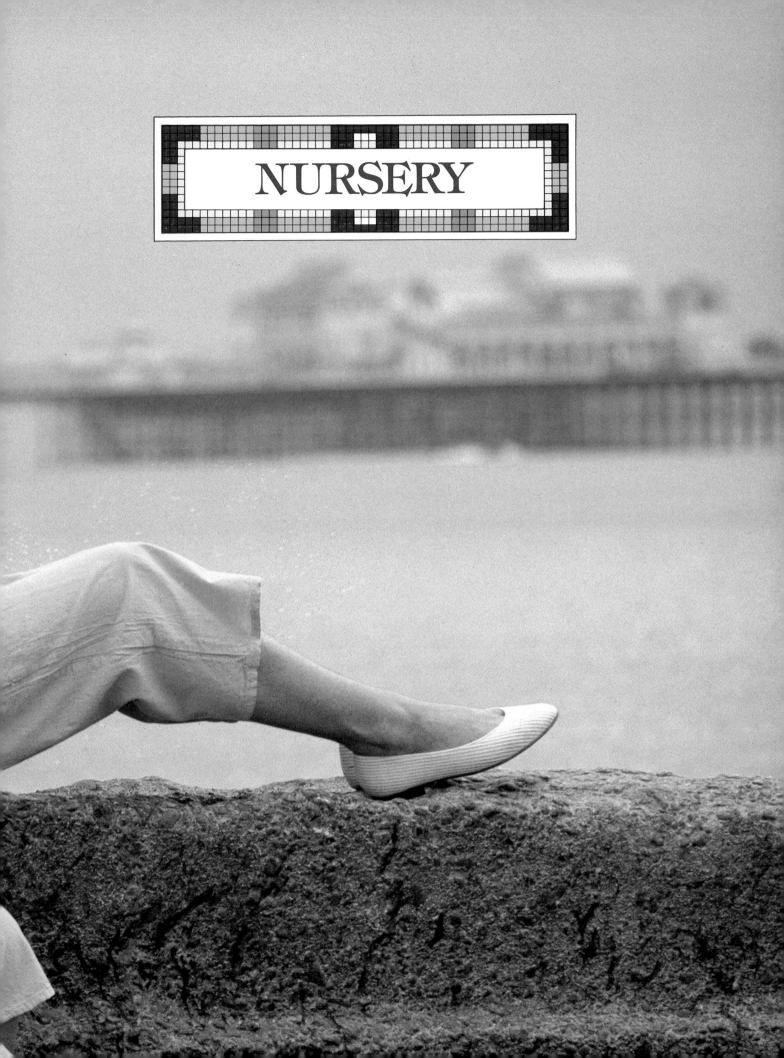

NURSERY

SUMMER SCOTTY

*Black and white Scotties on a grey ground form the pattern
for this short cotton cardie with three-quarter length sleeves.*

MATERIALS

Yarn
Use No. 8 cotton yarn.
Yarn A 250g *(grey)*
Yarn B 100g *(black)*
Yarn C 100g *(white)*
Yarn D 50g *(yellow)*
Yarn E 50g *(lilac)*

Needles
1 pair size 3¼mm
1 pair size 3mm
1 pair size 2¼mm

Notions
5 buttons
1m fine hat elastic

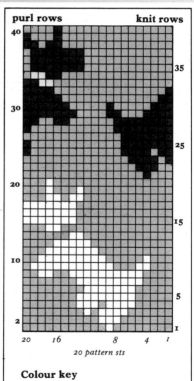

purl rows / knit rows

20 pattern sts

Colour key

grey

black

white

yellow

lilac

MEASUREMENTS

To fit bust 89 (96)cm (34, 36in).
(See also chart on p. 121.)

Tension
30 sts and 30 rows measure 10cm over
Scotty pattern on 3¼mm needles.

BACK

With 2¼mm needles and yarn A, cast on
124 (128) sts. Work 5cm in k1, p1 twisted
rib, increasing across the last wrong-side
row as follows: rib 2 (0) sts, *rib 9 (7) sts,
rib twice into the next st; repeat from *
11 (15) more times, rib 2 (0) sts – 136
(144) sts.
Change to 3¼mm needles and st st and
work Scotty pattern from chart, reading
odd (knit) rows from right to left and even
(purl) rows from left to right. Work the
pattern across knit rows as follows: *for the
smaller size (89cm)*, repeat the 20 pattern
sts (*1–20*) six times across the row and
then work sts *1–16* once to complete the
row; *for the larger size (94cm)*, repeat sts
1–20 seven times and then work sts *1–4*
once. Work purl rows in reverse. Continuing in pattern, work straight until you
have worked row 30 of the second working
of the pattern chart, and back measures
approximately 28cm from cast-on edge.
Shape armholes: Continuing in pattern,
cast off 6 sts at the beginning of the next
2 rows. Then k2 tog at each end of every
row until 100 (108) sts remain. Now work
straight in pattern until you have worked
row 6 (10) of the fourth working of the
pattern chart and back measures approximately 47 (48)cm from cast-on edge.
Shape shoulders: Cast off 6 sts at the
beginning of the next 4 rows. Then cast
off 6 (7) sts at the beginning of the next 6
rows. Divide the remaining 40 (42) sts in
half and transfer each half to a spare
needle or stitch holder.

Pocket linings

Begin by making pocket linings. With
3mm needles and yarn A, cast on 26 (28)
sts. Work 6cm in st st ending with a purl
row. Leave sts on a spare needle and make
another lining in the same way.

Left front

With 2¼mm needles and yarn A, cast on
56 (60) sts. Work 5cm in k1, p1 twisted
rib increasing across the last wrong-side
row as follows: rib 0 (2) sts, *rib 3 sts, rib
twice into the next st, rib 3 sts; repeat
from * seven more times,
rib 0 (2) – 64 (68) sts.

FRONTS

Change to 3¼mm needles and st st and
work pattern from chart. Work the pattern
across knit rows as follows: *for the smaller
size (89cm)*, repeat sts *1–20* three times
across the row and then work sts *1–4* to
finish the row; *for the larger size (94cm)*,
repeat sts *1–20* three times and then work
sts *1–8* once. Work purl rows in reverse.
Continue thus in pattern until you have
worked row 20 of the chart.
Pocket: Introduce pocket in row 21 as
follows: work the pattern across the first
19 (20) sts in the row, slip the next 26 (28)
sts on to a spare needle or stitch holder
and in their place work the pattern across
the 26 (28) sts of one pocket lining on
spare needle; continue pattern to end of
row. Continue in pattern until you have
worked row 22 of the second working of
the pattern chart and front measures
approximately 25cm.
Shape neck: Work the pattern
across the next row to the last 2 sts; k2
tog. Then work 3 rows straight. Now
work these four rows again – 62 (66) sts.
Shape armhole: Continuing in pattern,
cast off 6 sts at the beginning of the next
row, work pattern to last 2 sts, k2 tog.
Then continue to decrease one st at the
neck edge on every following 4th row, 13
(14) more times. *At the same time*,
decrease one st at the armhole edge on the
next 12 rows – 40 (44) sts. Now work
armhole edge straight, but continue to
decrease one st at the neck edge on every
4th row after previous decrease, as before,
10 (11) more times – 30 (33) sts. Then
work straight in pattern, until you have
worked row 6 (10) of the fourth working
of the pattern chart and the front measures
approximately 47 (48)cm from cast-
on edge.
Shape shoulder: Continuing in pattern,
cast off 6 sts at the beginning of the next
and following alternate row, then 6 (7)
sts at the beginning of the following 3
alternate rows.

Right front

Work in the same way as left front,
reverse pocket, armhole, neck and
shoulder shapings.

SLEEVES

With 2¼mm needles and yarn C, cast on 60 (64) sts. Work one row in k1, p1 twisted rib in yarn C. Join in yarn A and continue in rib for 7cm, increasing across the last (wrong-side) row as follows: rib 10 (12) sts, rib twice into the next 40 sts, rib 10 (12) sts – 100 (104) sts.

Change to 3¼mm needles and st st and work pattern from chart as follows: *for the smaller size,* repeat sts *1–20* five times; *for the larger size,* repeat sts *1–20* five times and then work sts *1–4* once. Work purl rows in reverse. Continue to work straight in pattern until you have worked row 30 of the second working of the pattern chart and the sleeve measures approximately 30cm from cast-on edge.

Shape top of sleeve: Continuing in pattern, cast off 6 (8) sts at the beginning of the next 2 rows. Then k2 tog at each end of the next and every following alternate row, ten times. Now work 14 (18) rows straight in pattern, and then k2 tog at each end of the next and every following alternate row 6 times. Then k2 tog at each end of the next 10 rows. Cast off the remaining 36 sts, to leave a wide edge which will be pleated into the armhole later.

Make another sleeve in the same way.

Join fronts to back at shoulders.

FRONT BANDS

Right front

With 2¼mm needles and yarn A, with right side of work facing and beginning at the lower edge, pick up and knit 81 sts up front opening edge as far as start of neck shaping; then pick up and knit a further 95 (99) sts around neck edge to centre-back, including the 21 (22) sts on first spare needle – 176 (180) sts. Work 3 rows of k1, p1 twisted rib.

Buttonholes: Make five buttonholes in the 4th row of ribbing as follows: rib 4 sts, *cast off 3 sts, rib 15 sts; repeat from * three more times, cast off 3 sts, rib to end of row. Work back along the next row (5th row) in rib, casting on 3 sts directly over those cast off in the previous row. Work 3 further rows in rib in yarn A. Join in yarn C and work one row of rib in yarn C. Cast off in rib in yarn C.

Left front

With 2¼mm needles and yarn A, beginning at the centre-back of neck with right side facing, rib the 21 (22) sts on remaining spare needle and then continue to pick up and knit 74 (77) sts around neck edge and a further 81 sts down front opening edge as far as hem edge. Work to correspond with right front band, omitting buttonholes.

POCKETS

Pocket tops

With 2¼mm needles and yarn A, with right side of work facing rib the 26 (28) sts of one pocket on spare needle. Work 9 rows in k1, p1 twisted rib in yarn A; join in yarn C and work a further row of rib in yarn C. Cast off in rib in yarn C.

TO MAKE UP

Press all pieces lightly from wrong side, avoiding ribbing. Join fronts to back at side seams. Join both underarm sleeve seams. Pin one sleeve into one armhole, matching side and sleeve seams and pleating the fullness around the top of the sleeve to fit armhole. Sew sleeve into armhole and repeat for other sleeve. Sew down sides of pocket tops and sew the three free sides of each pocket lining to the back of cardigan fronts. Join ribbing at centre-back. Sew on five buttons to left front band to correspond with buttonholes. Press seams lightly. Cut elastic to fit around bottom edge of cardigan and thread through the edge of the welt from wrong side, securing both ends.

BOYS ON BLUE

A long-sleeved Shetland cardigan with ribbed collar
which uses the same running boys motif
as for the sweater, but here the ground is of pale blue mix.

MATERIALS

Yarn
Use 2-ply jumper weight Shetland yarn.
Yarn A 200g *(pale blue mix)*
Yarn B 50g *(oat)*
Yarn C 50g *(black)*
Yarn D 25g *(red)*
Yarn E 25g *(green)*
Yarn F 25g *(mid-blue)*
Yarn G 25g *(yellow)*
Yarn H 25g *(rust)*
Yarn K 25g *(royal blue)*

Needles
1 pair size 3¼mm needles
1 pair size 2¾mm needles

Notions
8 buttons

BACK

With 2¾mm needles and yarn A, cast on
127 (135) sts. Work 5cm in k1, p1 twisted
rib in yarn A, increasing across the last
(wrong-side) row as follows: rib 4 (8) sts,
* rib 6 sts, rib twice into the next st;
repeat from * 16 more times, rib 4 (8) sts –
144 (152) sts.
Change to 3¼mm needles and st st and
work Boys pattern from chart, reading
odd (knit) rows from right to left and even
(purl) rows from left to right. Work the
pattern across knit rows as follows: *for the
smaller size* (91cm), repeat sts *1–25* five
times across the row, then work sts *1–19*
once to complete row; *for the larger size*
(97cm), repeat sts *1–25* six times, then
work sts *1–2* once to complete the row.
Work purl rows in reverse, working the
extra sts at the beginning of the row.
Continuing in pattern, work straight until
you have completed row 26 (30) of the
second working of the pattern chart and
the back measures approximately 36
(37)cm from the cast-on edge.
Shape armholes: Continuing in pattern,
cast off 10 (12) sts at the beginning of the
next 2 rows – 124 (128) sts. Then work
straight in pattern until you have worked
row 18 (26) of the third working of the
pattern chart, and the back measures
approximately 57 (59)cm.
Shape shoulders: Continuing in pattern,
cast off 14 sts at the beginning of the next
4 rows. Then cast off 11 (12) sts at the
beginning of the following 2 rows. Cast off
remaining 46 (48) sts.

FRONTS

Left front
With 2¾mm needles and yarn A, cast on
64 (68) sts. Work 5cm in k1, p1 twisted
rib in yarn A, increasing across the last
(wrong-side) row as follows: rib 2 sts, *rib
11 (12) sts, rib twice into the next st;
repeat from * four more times, rib 2 (1)
sts – 69 (73) sts.

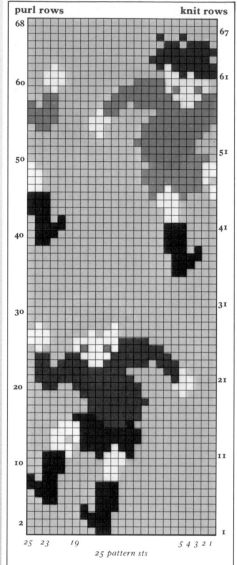

purl rows   knit rows

25 pattern sts

25 23   19   5 4 3 2 1

Colour key

pale blue mix   mid-blue

oat   yellow

black   rust

red   royal blue

green

Change to 3¼mm needles and st st and
work Boys pattern from chart. Work
the pattern across knit rows as follows:
for the smaller size, work sts *5–25* once,
then work sts *1–25* once, and finish the
row with sts *1–23*; *for the larger size*,
work sts *3–25* once, then work sts *1–25*
twice. Work purl rows in reverse (i.e.
small size, work sts *23–1, 25–1, 25–5*;
large size, work sts *25–1* twice and *25–3*
once). Continuing in pattern, work
straight until you have worked row 26 (30)
of the second working of the pattern chart
and the front measures approximately 36
(37)cm from the cast-on edge.
Shape armhole: Continuing in pattern,
cast off 10 (12) sts at the beginning of the
next row – 59 (61) sts. Then work straight
in pattern until you have worked row 65
of the second working of the pattern chart
(row 5 of the third working of the pattern
chart) and front measures approximately
49 (52)cm from cast-on edge.
Shape neck: Cast off 4 sts at the beginning of the next row. Then k2 tog at the
neck edge on every following row, 16 (17)
times – 39 (40) sts remain. Now work
straight until you have worked row 18 (26)
of the third working of the pattern chart
and front measures approximately 56
(58)cm from the cast-on edge.
Shape shoulder: Continuing in pattern,
cast off 14 sts at the beginning of the next
and following alternate row. Work one
row straight. Then cast off 11 (12) sts at
the beginning of the next row.

Right front
Work in the same way as left front,
but reverse armhole, neck
and shoulder shapings.

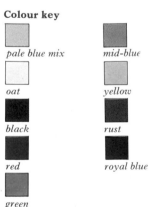

SLEEVES

With 2¾mm needles and yarn A, cast on 60 (64) sts. Work 10cm in k1, p1 twisted rib, increasing across the last (wrong-side) row as follows: rib 0 (2) sts, *rib 3 sts, rib twice into the next st; repeat from * 14 (14) more times, rib 0 (2) sts – 75 (79) sts. Change to 3¼mm needles and st st and work Fair Isle pattern from chart. Work the pattern across knit rows as follows: *for the smaller size,* work sts *1–25* three times; *for the larger size,* work sts *1–25* three times and then work sts *1–4* to finish the row. Work purl rows in reverse. Continuing thus in pattern, shape the sides by increasing one st at each end of the 3rd and every following 4th row until there are 129 (135) sts on the needle. Take the extra sts into the pattern as they are made. Then work straight until you have worked row 66 of the second working of the pattern chart and the sleeve measures approximately 54cm from the cast-on edge. Cast off right across; this cast-off edge should measure 41 (43)cm to fit into armhole.

Make another sleeve in the same way.

FRONT BANDS

Right front

With 2¾mm needles and yarn A, beginning at the lower edge of right front with right side facing.

pick up and knit 143 (151) sts up front opening edge to start of neck shaping. Work 3 rows in k1, p1 twisted rib.
Buttonholes: Make 5 buttonholes in the fourth row of ribbing as follows: rib 4 (5) sts, *cast off 3 sts, rib 16 (17) sts; repeat from * six more times, cast off 3 sts, rib 3 sts. Rib back across row 5, casting on 3 sts directly over those cast off in the previous row. Work a further 4 rows in rib in yarn A. Join in yarn F and work one more row in yarn F. Cast off in rib in yarn F.

Left front

With right side of work facing, using 2¾mm needles and yarn A, beginning at the start of the neck shaping, pick up and knit 143 (151) sts down left front opening edge to hem edge. Finish to correspond with right front band, omitting buttonholes.

COLLAR

With 2¾mm needles and yarn A, cast on 113 (115) sts. Work one row in k1, p1 twisted rib. Continuing in rib in yarn A, increase one st at each end of the next and following 5 alternate rows. Then increase one st at each end of the next 6 rows – 137 (139) sts. Work 4 rows in rib without shaping. Now decrease one st at each end of the next 6 rows, then decrease one st at each end of the next and following 5 alternate rows. Work one row in rib. Cast off in rib.

TO MAKE UP

Press all pieces lightly from wrong side, avoiding ribbing. Join fronts to back at side and shoulder seams. Join underarm sleeve seams, leaving 3 (4)cm unstitched at top of seam. Pin the cast-off edge around the top of the sleeve into the top of the armhole, and pin each side of the unstitched section of the sleeve seam across the straight cast-off edge at the base of the armhole. Sew sleeve in position and repeat for other sleeve.

Pin cast-on edge of collar around neck edge, starting and ending at the points where the front bands start. Stitch collar to neck and then fold the collar in half so that the cast-off edge just covers the seam of the cast-on edge. Pin in position and then slip neatly in place so that seam is covered. Sew buttons to left front band to correspond with buttonholes. Press seams lightly from wrong side.

MEASUREMENTS

To fit chest 91 (97)cm (36, 38in).
(See also chart on p. 121.)
Tension
32 sts and 30 rows measure 10cm over Boys pattern on 3¼mm needles.

TEDDY·BEAR

*Teddy-bears are the basis of this nursery pattern waistcoat.
The bears are worked against a plain ground which is bordered
with dark brown rib; the back is worked in striped rib.*

MEASUREMENTS

To fit chest 86 (91)cm (34, 36in).
(See also chart on p. 121.)
Tension
32 sts and 30 rows measure 10cm over
Teddy-Bear pattern on 3¼mm needles.

MATERIALS

Yarn
Use 2-ply jumper weight Shetland yarn
throughout. Different sizes will require
different quantities of main yarns.
Yarn A 75 (100)g *(dark fawn)*
Yarn B 75 (100)g *(chocolate)*
Yarn C 25g *(red)*
Yarn D 25g *(violet)*

Yarn E 50g *(mid brown)*
Yarn F 25g *(jade mix)*
Yarn G 25g *(mid blue)*
Needles
1 pair size 3¼mm
1 pair size 3mm
1 pair size 2¾mm
Notions
5 × 1.5cm buttons

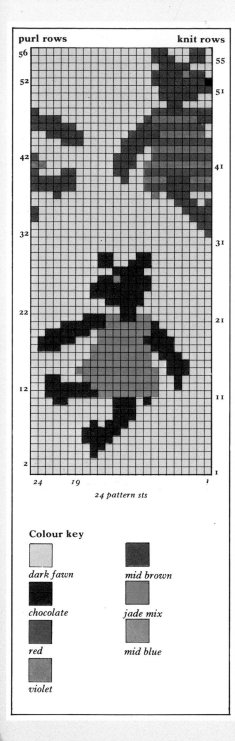

purl rows   **knit rows**

56
55
52
51

42
41

32
31

22
21

12
11

2
1

24   19   1

24 pattern sts

Colour key

dark fawn   mid brown

chocolate   jade mix

red   mid blue

violet

FRONTS

Left front

With 2¾mm needles and yarn B, cast on 70 (76) sts. Work 5cm in k1, p1 twisted rib in yarn B, increasing one st at each end of the final (wrong-side) row – 72 (78) sts. Change to 3¼mm needles and st st and work Teddy bear pattern from chart, reading odd (knit) rows from right to left and even (purl) rows from left to right. Work the pattern across knit rows as follows: *for the smaller size* (91cm), repeat sts *1–24* three times; *for the larger size*, work sts *19–24* once, and then repeat sts *1–24* three times. Work purl rows in reverse. Continue in pattern until you have worked row 24 (28) of the second working of the pattern chart and the front measures approximately 31 (33)cm from cast-on edge.

Shape armhole and neck: Continuing in pattern, cast off 10 (12) sts at the beginning of the next row, then work pattern across to the last 2 sts; k2 tog. Continuing in pattern, decrease one st at the armhole edge on the next 18 (19) rows; then work armhole edge straight. *At the same time,* continue to decrease one st at neck edge on every following 4th row after the first decrease, 15 (16) times – 28 (30) sts remain. Then work neck edge straight until you have completed row 36 (42) of the third working of pattern chart and front measures approximately 54 (56)cm from cast-on edge.

Shape shoulder: Cast off 10 sts at the beginning of the next row. Then cast off 9 (10) sts at the beginning of the following 2 alternate rows.

Right front

Work in the same way as left front, but reverse armhole, neck and shoulder shapings.

BACK

With 2¾mm needles and yarn B, cast on 140 (152) sts. Work 5cm in k1, p1 twisted rib, increasing 4 sts across the last (wrong-side) row by working twice into every 35th (38th) st, 4 times in all – 144 (156) sts. Change to 3mm needles and continue to work entire back in twisted rib in the following three-colour stripe sequence:

back of waistcoat

Row 1: Yarn E
Row 2: Yarn A
Row 3: Yarn B
Carry yarns not in use up the sides of the work until required. Work straight until back measures approximately 31 (33)cm from cast-on edge to start of armhole shaping.

Shape armholes: With right side facing, cast off 3 (4) sts at the beginning of the next 2 rows. Then k2 tog at each end of every row until 104 (110) sts remain. Work armhole edges straight until back measures approximately 54 (56)cm and matches fronts from cast-on edge to start of shoulder shaping.

Shape shoulders: With right side of work facing, cast off 10 sts at the beginning of the next 2 rows; then cast off 9 (10) sts at the beginning of the following 4 rows. Divide the remaining 48 (50) sts equally in half and transfer each half to a spare needle or stitch holder.

Join fronts to back at shoulders.

FRONT BANDS

Right front

Using 2¾mm needles and yarn B and with the right side of the work facing, beginning at lower edge, pick up and knit 101 (105) sts up right front opening edge as far as start of neck shaping. Then continue to pick up and knit 84 (88) sts around neck edge as far as centre-back, including the 24 (25) sts on the first spare needle – 185 (193) sts in all. Work 3 rows of k1, p1 twisted rib in yarn B.

Buttonholes: Make 5 buttonholes in the 4th row of ribbing as follows: rib 4 sts, cast off 3 sts, rib 20 (21) sts; repeat from * 3 more times, cast off 3 sts and then rib to end of row. Rib back across the next row (row 5) as before, but cast on 3 sts directly over those cast off in the previous row. Then work 4 more rows in rib in yarn B. Join in yarn E and work one row in rib in yarn E. Cast off in yarn E.

Left front

Beginning at the centre-back with yarn B, rib the 24 (25) sts on the remaining spare needle; then pick up and knit 60 (63) sts around neck edge to start of neck shaping and a further 101 (105) sts down front to lower edge. Work to correspond with right front band, but omit buttonholes.

ARMHOLE BANDS

With 2¾mm needles and yarn B and with the right side of the work facing, pick up and knit 155 (163) sts around one armhole. Work to correspond with left front band. Repeat for other armhole.

TO MAKE UP

Join fronts to back at either side as for shoulders. Press Fair Isle parts and seams carefully from wrong side, avoiding all ribbing. Join ribbing at back of neck. Sew on the 5 buttons to left front band to correspond with buttonholes.

SEAGULLS

Seagulls sweeping against a blue sky lend this boat neck sweater a nautical flavour. It is an ideal sailing pullover for men or women.

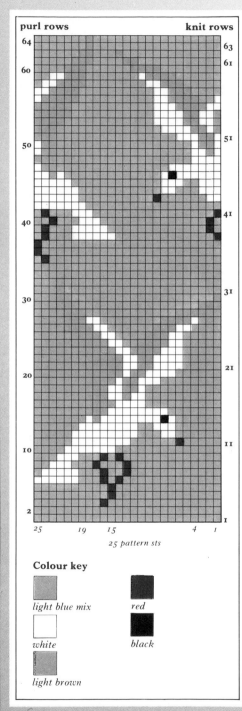

purl rows **knit rows**

64 — 63
60 — 61
50 — 51
40 — 41
30 — 31
20 — 21
10 — 11
2 — 1

25 19 15 4 1
25 pattern sts

Colour key

light blue mix

white

light brown

red

black

MATERIALS

Yarn
Use 2-ply jumper weight Shetland yarn.
Different sizes require different quantities
of yarn.
Yarn A 175 (175, 200)g *(light blue mix)*
Yarn B 100g *(white)*
Yarn C 100 (100, 125)g *(light brown)*
Yarn D 25g *(red)*
Yarn E 25g *(black)*
Needles
1 pair size 3¼mm
1 pair size 2¼mm

MEASUREMENTS

To fit chest 91 (97, 107)cm (36, 38, 42in).
(See also chart on p. 122.)
Tension
32 sts and 32 rows measure 10cm over
Seagull pattern on 3¼mm needles.

BACK and FRONT

Work the back and front in the same way.
With 2¼mm needles and yarn C, cast on
130 (136, 149) sts. Work 8cm in k1, p1
twisted rib, increasing across the last
wrong-side row as follows: rib 2 (5, 10)
sts, *rib twice into the next st, rib 8 (6, 4)
sts; repeat from * 13 (17, 25) more times,
rib 2 (5, 9) sts – 144 (154, 175) sts.
Change to 3¼mm needles and st st and
work Seagull pattern from chart, reading
odd (knit) rows from right to left and even
(purl) rows from left to right. Work the
pattern across knit rows as follows: *for the
small size* (91cm), repeat sts *1–25* five
times across the row and then work sts
1–19 once to complete row; *for the
medium size* (97cm), repeat sts *1–25* six
times and then work sts *1–4* once; *for the
large size*, repeat sts *1–25* seven times.
Work purl rows in reverse. Continue thus
in pattern until you have worked row 26
(26, 46) of the second working of the
pattern chart and the work measures
approximately 36 (36, 42)cm from cast-
on edge.
Shape armholes: Continuing in pattern,
cast off 10 (12, 16) sts at the beginning of
the next 2 rows – 124 (130, 141) sts. Then
work straight in pattern until you have
worked row 64 (2, 34) of the second
(third, third) working of the pattern chart
and the work measures approximately 48
(48, 58)cm from cast-on edge. Join in yarn
C and work top yoke in yarn C as follows:
knit one row, then work 11cm in k1, p1
twisted rib, ending with a wrong-side row.
Join in yarn B, and work the next (right-
side) row in rib in yarn B. Cast off in rib
in yarn B.

SLEEVES

With 2¼mm needles and yarn B, cast on
60 (62, 71) sts. Work one row in k1, p1
twisted rib in yarn B. Join in yarn C and
work a further 10 (11, 11)cm in twisted rib
in yarn C, increasing across the last
wrong-side row as follows: rib 2 (2, 7) sts,
*rib 2 sts, rib twice into the next st;
repeat from * eighteen more times, rib 1
(1, 7) sts – 79 (79, 90) sts.
Change to 3¼mm needles and st st and
work Seagull pattern from chart. Work
the pattern across knit rows as follows: *for
the small and medium sizes*, repeat sts *1–25*
three times, then work sts *1–4* once; *for
the large size*, work sts *1–25* three times,
then work sts *1–15* once. Work purl rows
in reverse. Continue thus in pattern, *at the
same time*, shaping the sides by increasing
one st at each end of the 3rd and every
following 4th row until there are 135
(139, 148) sts on the needle. Take the
extra sts into the pattern as they are made.
Then work straight in pattern until you
have completed the second working of the
pattern chart. *For the large size only*, work
an extra 2 rows in st st and yarn A only.
The sleeve should now measure approximately 50 (50, 51)cm from the cast-on
edge. Cast off right across row, fairly
loosely; this cast-off edge should measure
approximately 43 (46, 49)cm to fit into
armhole.

TO MAKE UP

Press all pieces lightly from wrong side,
avoiding ribbing. Join front to back at
side seams. Overlap the edge of the front
neck welt and the back neck welt by 2cm
and hold each side with a pin. Lift the
front welt slightly and sew the underneath
of the front welt to the back welt for about
5cm from outside shoulder edge, so that
stitches do not show on right side. Repeat
for other shoulder. Join sleeve seams,
leaving 3 (4, 5)cm of sleeve seam unstitched at top of seam. Pin top of sleeve
into top of armhole and pin either side of
the unstitched section of sleeve seam
across the straight cast-off edge at the
bottom of armhole. Sew in position and
repeat for other sleeve. Press seams lightly
from wrong side.

STARING CATS

Black Cats with eager yellow eyes on a ground of pink and blue form the pattern for this men's or women's loose-fitting crew neck sweater.

MEASUREMENTS

To fit chest 86 (91, 97, 101)cm (34, 36, 38, 40in).
(See also chart on p. 122.)

Tension

32 sts and 30 rows measure 10cm over Cats pattern on 3¼mm needles.

MATERIALS

Yarn

Use 2-ply jumper weight Shetland yarn. Different sizes require different quantities of yarn.

Yarn A 200 (200, 200, 225)g *(red/blue mix)*
Yarn B 100 (100, 100, 125)g *(mid-blue mix)*
Yarn C 75 (75, 75, 100)g *(ivory)*
Yarn D 75 (75, 85, 100)g *(black)*
Yarn E 25 (25, 25, 50)g *(rust)*
Yarn F 25 (25, 25, 50)g *(yellow)*

Needles

1 pair size 3¼mm
1 pair size 2¾mm

BACK

**With 2¾mm needles and yarn A, cast on 120 (128, 138, 148) sts. Work 5 (5, 6, 6)cm in k1, p1 twisted rib in yarn A, increasing across the last (wrong-side) row as follows: rib 0 (9, 3, 8) sts, *rib 5 (4, 5, 5) sts, rib twice into the next st; repeat from * 19 (21, 21, 21) more times, rib 0 (9, 3, 8) sts – 140 (150, 160, 170) sts in all.

Change to 3¼mm needles and st st and work Cats pattern from chart, reading odd (knit) rows from right to left and even (purl) rows from left to right. Work the pattern across knit rows as follows: *for size 89cm*, repeat the basic 20 pattern sts seven times across the row; *for size 94cm*, repeat sts *1–20*, seven times across the row and then work sts *1–10* once; *for size 99cm*, work sts *1–20*, eight times across the row; *for size 104cm*, work sts *1–20*, eight times across the row and then work sts *1–10* once. Work purl rows in reverse. Continue to work pattern thus, until you have worked row 20 (24, 24, 28) of the third working of the pattern chart and back measures approximately 42 (43, 44, 46)cm.

Shape armholes: Cast off 12 (13, 14, 15) sts at the beginning of the next 2 rows. ** Then work straight in pattern until you have worked row 38 (46, 46, 46) of the fourth working of the pattern chart and back measures approximately 63 (66, 67, 67)cm. *For the larger size* (size 104cm), continue in st st and yarn A only (to avoid having a broken pattern at shoulder edge) until back measures 68cm from cast-on edge, ending on a wrong-side row. Then continue as follows for all sizes.

Shape shoulders: Cast off 13 (14, 15, 15) sts at the beginning of the next 2 rows. Then cast off 11 (12, 13, 14) sts at the beginning of the next 4 rows. Leave the remaining 46 (48, 50, 54) sts on a spare needle or stitch holder.

FRONT

Work as for back from ** to ** – 116 (124, 132, 140) sts. Continuing in pattern work straight until you have worked row 14 (18, 18, 22) of the fourth working of the pattern chart, and front measures approximately 55 (56, 57, 59)cm from the cast-on edge.

Shape neck: On the next row, work the first 43 (46, 49, 52) sts of the row in the pattern and then turn, leaving the remaining 73 (78, 83, 88) sts on a spare needle. Continue to work pattern on these 43 (46, 49, 52) sts and decrease one st at the neck edge on the next 8 (8, 8, 9) rows – 35 (38, 41, 43) sts remain. Then work neck edge straight, continuing in pattern for the two smaller sizes and working a few rows in yarn A for the two larger sizes, until the front measures the same as the back from the cast-on edge to the start of the shoulder shaping, ending on a wrong-side row – approximately 63 (66, 67, 68)cm.

Shape shoulder: Cast off 13 (14, 15, 15) sts at the beginning of the next row. Then cast off 11 (12, 13, 14) sts at the beginning of the following two alternate rows, so completing left shoulder edge.

Rejoin yarn to remaining sts on spare

needle. Cast off the first 30 (32, 34, 36) sts to form neck edge and then work the pattern to the end of the row. Finish right shoulder to correspond with left shoulder, reversing neck and shoulder shapings.

SLEEVES

With 2¾mm needles and yarn A, cast on 58 (60, 62, 64) sts. Work 10cm in k1, p1 twisted rib in yarn A. Increase across the next wrong-side row as follows: rib 10 sts, rib twice into each of the next 38 (40, 42, 44) sts, rib 10 sts – 96 (100, 104, 108) sts in all.
Change to 3¼mm needles and st st and work the next 8 rows in the following stripe sequence:
Row 1: (Yarn D) knit.
Row 2: (Yarn F) purl.
Row 3: (Yarn E) knit.
Row 4: (Yarn D) purl.
Row 5: (Yarn F) knit.
Row 6: (Yarn E) purl.
Row 7: (Yarn D) knit.
Row 8: (Yarn A) purl.
Then continue to work sleeve in st st in yarn A only. Shape sides by increasing one st at each end of the next and every following 8th row until there are 116 (124, 132, 140) sts on the needle. Then work straight until sleeve measures 52 (52, 54, 54)cm from the cast-on edge. Cast off right across this edge, taking into account that this edge should measure approximately 40 (43, 46, 48)cm to fit armhole. Make another sleeve in the same way.

NECKBAND

Join right shoulder seam.
With 2¾mm needles and yarn A, beginning at left shoulder, pick up and knit 27 (29, 31, 33) sts down left side of neck, 28 (30, 32, 34) sts across centre-front cast-off edge, 27 (29, 31, 33) sts up right side of neck to right shoulder seam, and then the 46 (48, 50, 54) sts on the spare needle at the back of the neck – 128 (136, 144, 154) sts in all. Work 12 rows in k1, p1 twisted rib in yarn A. Cast off in rib in yarn A.

TO MAKE UP

Press all pieces lightly from the wrong side, avoiding ribbing. Join left shoulder seam and neckband. Join side seams and sleeve seams, leaving 4 (4, 4, 5)cm unstitched at the top of the sleeve seam. (This unstitched section will then fit straight cast-off edge at the bottom of the armhole.) Pin cast-off edge of sleeve top into top of armhole easing edges if necessary, and pin the unstitched sides of the sleeve seam across the straight edge at the bottom of the armhole. Sew in position and repeat for other sleeve. Press seams from wrong side.

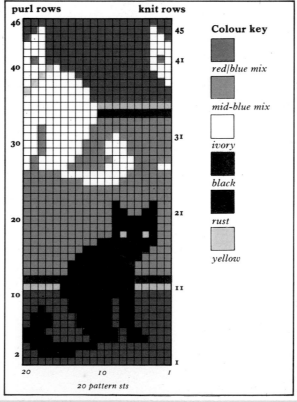

purl rows   **knit rows**

Colour key

red/blue mix

mid-blue mix

ivory

black

rust

yellow

20 pattern sts

BOYS ON BLACK

*This crew neck sweater uses the running boys motif,
set here against a black background which emphasises the pattern.
The neck and cuff ribbing are edged with contrasting yarn.*

MATERIALS

Yarn

Use 2-ply jumper weight Shetland yarn.
Yarn A 225g *(black)*
Yarn B 50g *(bluebell)*
Yarn C 25g *(rust)*
Yarn D 25g *(yellow)*
Yarn E 25g *(red)*
Yarn F 25g *(leaf green)*
Yarn G 25g *(sand)*

Needles

1 pair size 3¼mm
1 pair size 3mm
1 pair size 2¾mm
1 set of four size 2¾mm double-pointed needles *or* 2¾mm circular needle.

MEASUREMENTS

To fit chest 86–91 (97–102)cm (34–36, 38–40in).
(See also chart on p. 122.)

Tension

30 sts and 28 rows measure 10cm over Fair Isle pattern on 3¼mm needles.

BACK

**With 2¾mm needles and yarn A, cast on 135 (150) sts. Work 5cm in k1, p1 twisted rib in yarn A, increasing across the last (wrong-side) row as follows: *p8 (5), purl twice into the next st; repeat from * to end of row – 150 (175) sts.
Change to 3¼mm needles and st st and work Fair Isle pattern from chart, reading odd (knit) rows from right to left and even (purl) rows from left to right. Repeat the 25 pattern sts six (seven) times across the rows. Continue straight in pattern until you have worked row 38 (42) of the second working of the pattern chart, and the back measures approximately 43 (45)cm from cast-on edge.
Shape armholes: Continuing in pattern, cast off 10 (15) sts at the beginning of the next 2 rows** – 130 (145) sts. Then work straight until you have worked row 28 (36) of the third working of the pattern chart and work measures approximately 64 (67)cm from cast-on edge.
Shape shoulders: Continuing in pattern, cast off 15 sts at the beginning of the next 2 rows. Then cast off 13 (15) sts at the beginning of the next 4 rows. Transfer the remaining 48 (55) sts to a spare needle or stitch holder.

FRONT

Work as for back from ** to ** – 130 (145) sts. Then work straight in pattern until you have worked row 68 of the second working of the pattern chart (row 8 of the third working of the pattern chart) and front measures approximately 54 (57)cm from cast-on edge.
Shape neck: On the next (right-side) row, work the first 47 (53) sts of the pattern, and transfer them to a spare needle or stitch holder; then cast off the next 36 (39) sts; continue in pattern across remaining 47 (53) sts of row. Con-

tinue to shape neck on these last 47 (53) sts, decreasing one st at the neck edge on the next 6 rows. Then work straight in pattern on these remaining sts until the right front measures the same as the back from the cast-on edge to start of shoulder shaping – approximately 64 (67)cm.
Shape shoulders: With wrong side facing, cast off 15 (17) sts at beginning of next row, then cast off 13 (15) sts at beginning of the following 2 alternate rows. With wrong side facing, rejoin yarn to the 47 (53) sts of the left front on the remaining spare needle at neck edge. Work left front to correspond with right front, reversing the neck and shoulder shapings.

SLEEVES

With 2¾mm needles and yarn C, cast on 60 (66) sts and work one row in k1, p1 twisted rib in yarn C. Join in yarn A and continue in twisted rib until the work measures 9cm.
Change to 3¼mm needles and work the entire sleeve in st st and yarn A. Shape sides of sleeve by increasing one st at the end of the first and every following 4th row, until there are 130 (136) sts on the needle. Then work a few rows straight until the sleeve measures 53cm from the cast-on edge. Cast off fairly loosely across the row. (This cast-off edge across top of sleeve joins with the straight edge around the top of the armhole. The last 4 (5)cm of underarm sleeve seam will join with the 10 (15) cast-off sts at the bottom of the armhole.)
Make another sleeve in the same way.

NECKBAND

Join front to back at the shoulders. Using the four 2¾mm double-pointed needles or circular needle, beginning at the left shoulder seam and using yarn A, pick up and knit 33 sts down left side of the neck, 34 (37) sts across the cast-off edge at centre-front, 33 sts up the right side of the neck and finally the 48 (55) sts from the spare needle at the back of the neck – 148 (158) sts in all. Then work 10 rounds in k1, p1 twisted rib in yarn A. Join in yarn C and work one further round of twisted rib in yarn C. Cast off in rib in yarn C.

TO MAKE UP

Press all pieces carefully from the wrong side, avoiding ribbing. Join front to back at the side seams. Join sleeve seams in the same way, leaving the last 4 (5)cm at the top of the seam unstitched. Pin the straight cast-off edge at the top of the sleeve into the top of the armhole, easing sleeve head if necessary; pin either side of the unstitched 4 (5)cm of sleeve seam across straight cast-off edge at the bottom of armhole. Sew in position and repeat for other sleeve. Press seams.

purl rows   knit rows

25 pattern sts

Colour key

black   red

bluebell   leaf green

rust   sand

yellow

BUTTERFLIES

*Blue and yellow Butterflies against meadow shades of green and beige
form the pattern of this one-size waistcoat. The waistcoat is worked in one piece
as far as the armholes and bordered with cable pattern.*

MATERIALS

Yarn
Use 2-ply jumper weight Shetland yarn.
Yarn A 125g *(olive mix)*
Yarn B 75g *(light brown)*
Yarn C 75g *(mustard)*
Yarn D 75g *(light blue)*
Yarn E 25g *(bright blue)*
Yarn F 25g *(orange mix)*
Yarn G 75g *(chocolate)*
Yarn H 100g *(oat)*

Needles
1 pair size 3¾mm
1 pair size 3¼mm
1 circular 3¼mm needle
1 circular 2¾mm needle
1 cable needle

Notions
5 × 1.5cm buttons

MEASUREMENTS

One-size: to fit chest 91–97cm (36–38in).
(See also chart on p. 122.)

Tension
32 sts and 32 rows measure 10cm over
Fair Isle pattern on 3¼mm needles.
Note: The front and back of the waistcoat
are knitted in one piece using a circular
needle, until the start of the armhole
shaping; knit as usual in rows.

BACK and FRONTS

With the 2¾mm circular needle and yarn
A, cast on 284 sts. Work 10cm in k1, p1
twisted rib in yarn A. On the last (wrong-
side) row, increase as follows: *p9, purl
twice into the next st, p4; repeat from *
across row until last 4 sts; p4 – 304 sts in all.
Change to the 3¼mm circular needle and
st st and work pattern from chart. Read
odd (knit) rows from right to left and even
(purl) rows from left to right. Work the
extra 2 sts indicated (sts *1–2*) at the beginning of knit rows; then work the basic 30
sts (sts *3–32*) indicated, ten times across
the row and finish the row with sts *33* and
34. Work purl rows in reverse, starting
with sts *34–33* and finishing with sts *2–1*.
Continue thus in pattern until you have
completed row 64 of first working of
pattern chart, and the work measures
approximately 30cm from cast-on edge.

Shape neck and armhole: To shape
neck edge k2 tog at each of the next and
every following 3rd row. *At the same time,*
when you have completed row 16 of the
second working of the pattern chart and
the work measures approximately 37cm
from cast-on edge, divide work for armholes as follows: on the next row, change
to the pair of 3¼mm needles and work the
first 65 sts of the row, then turn, leaving
the remaining sts in the row on a spare
needle.

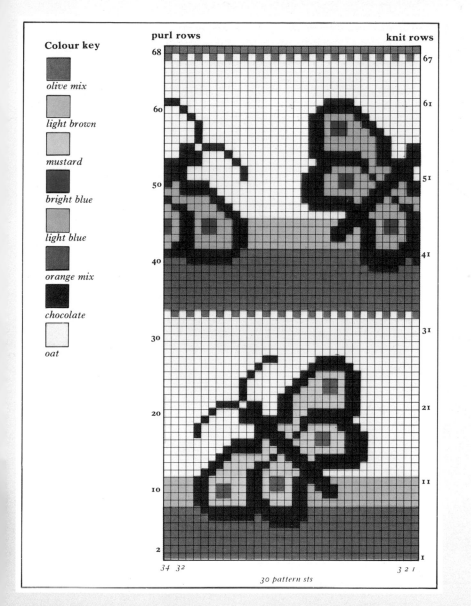

Colour key

olive mix

light brown

mustard

bright blue

light blue

orange mix

chocolate

oat

68

60

50

40

30

20

10

2

67

61

51

41

31

21

11

1

34   32   3 2 1

30 pattern sts

Row 9: Knit

Row 10: K3, p6, k3

These 10 rows form the cable pattern. Work rows 1–4 again.

Buttonholes: Make 4 buttonholes in the next row as follows:

Row 5: *K5, cast off 2, k5

Row 6: K3, p2, cast on 2, p2, k3

Then work 28 rows straight in cable pattern*. Repeat from * to * twice more, then make one more buttonhole in the next 2 rows as before.

Continue straight in cable pattern (repeating rows 1–10 and omitting buttonholes), until strip is long enough to fit from lower edge, up right front, around back of neck and down left front, slightly stretching the strip as you measure. Then cast off.

Armholes

With 3¾mm needles and yarn A, cast on 12 sts. Work rows 1–10 of the cable pattern as before, repeating them until the strip measures 51cm. Then cast off. Make another strip in the same way.

TO MAKE UP

Press the waistcoat lightly from the back avoiding all ribbing.

Front borders: Pin cable strip around front opening edges and neck, so that the top buttonhole is just below the start of the neck shaping on the right front. Attach to main body of waistcoat with a flat seam sewn from the wrong side. Sew five buttons to left front border, to match buttonholes.

Armhole borders: Overlap the short ends of one armhole border piece, so right sides of both ends face uppermost, to form a 'V' (see p. 140). Hold a pin and then neatly sew around the sides of the overlapping ends to hold them together. Pin the complete cable strip around one armhole, with right sides together, fitting the point of the 'V' where the ends join into the base of the armhole. Oversew borders to main work sewing from the wrong side with matching yarn. Repeat for other armhole, and press seams lightly from wrong side.

Right front

Continuing in pattern on these first 65 sts, decrease one st at the front edge on the next and every following 3rd row, as before, until 40 sts remain. Then work straight until you have completed row 27 of the third working of pattern chart, and the front measures approximately 61cm from the cast-on edge. With the wrong side facing, cast off right across the row. Now turn to the remaining sts on the spare needle. Work the next 160 sts in the row (row 17). Then turn, leaving the remaining 65 sts on a spare needle. Work the pattern across the 160 sts to form back. Continue in pattern until you have worked row 28 of the third working of the pattern chart, and back measures approximately 61cm from the cast-on edge. Then cast off.

Left front

With right side of work facing join the yarn to remaining 65 sts on spare needle. Work across row (row 17 of pattern chart) from armhole edge to neck edge, shaping neck edge in the same way as for right front. Work to correspond with right front, ending with row 27 of the third working of the pattern chart and reversing neck shaping. Cast off across row.

CABLE BORDERS

Note: To work the instruction 'cable 6' (see row 7 below), slip the next 3 sts in the row on to a cable needle and hold to the front of the work; knit the next 3 sts, then knit the 3 sts from the cable needle.

Join fronts to back at shoulder seams.

Fronts

With 3¾mm needles and yarn A, cast on 12 sts. Then work border as follows:

Row 1: Knit

Row 2: K3, p6, k3

Row 3: Knit

Row 4: K3, p6, k3

Row 5: Knit

Row 6: K3, p6, k3

Row 7: K3, cable 6, k3

Row 8: K3, p6, k3

DACHSHUND

Busy Dachshunds trot across the fronts of this dashing waistcoat,
which has two front pockets and a striped rib back. The background colour
could be lightened to give a more distinctive pattern.

MATERIALS

Yarn
Use 2-ply jumper weight Shetland yarn.
Yarn A 100g *(sand)*
Yarn B 100g *(rust/blue mix)*
Yarn C 50 g *(chocolate)*
Yarn D 25g *(mid-brown mix)*
Yarn E 25g *(rust)*
Needles
1 pair size 3¼mm
1 pair size 3mm
1 pair size 2¾mm
Notions
5 buttons

MEASUREMENTS

To fit chest 84 (91, 99)cm (33, 36, 39in).
(See also chart on p. 122.)
Tension
32 sts and 30 rows measure 10cm over
Dachshund pattern on 3¼mm needles.

FRONTS

Left front
With 2¾mm needles and yarn B, cast on
66 (72, 78) sts. Work 5cm in k1, p1
twisted rib in yarn B.
Change to 3¼mm needles and st st and
work the Dachshund pattern from the
chart, reading odd (knit) rows from right
to left and even (purl) rows from left to
right. Work the pattern across knit rows
as follows: *for the small size* (84cm), work
sts 1–36 once and then work sts 1–30 once
to finish the row; *for the medium size*
(91cm), repeat sts 1–36 twice; *for the
large size* (99cm), repeat sts 1–36 twice
and then work sts 1–6 once to finish
the row. Work purl rows in reverse.
Continue thus in pattern until you have
completed row 16 of the pattern chart.
Pocket: Introduce pocket in the next row
(row 17) as follows: work the first 19 (20,
21) sts of the row, cast off the next 28
(32, 36) sts and then work the pattern to
the end of the row. On the next row (row
18), work the pattern across the first 19
(20, 21) sts in the row, cast on 28 (32, 36)
sts over those cast off in the previous row
and then work the pattern to the end of
the row.
Work straight in pattern until you have
worked row 10 (14, 18) of the third working of the pattern chart and the front
measures approximately 30 (31, 32)cm.
Shape armhole and neck: Cast off 12
(13, 14) sts at the beginning of the next
row (row 11, 15, 19 of chart); then work
pattern to the last 2 sts; k2 tog. Continuing in pattern, decrease one st at the armhole edge on the next 15 (16, 17) rows.
Then work armhole edge straight. *At the
same time,* continue to decrease one st at
the neck edge on every following 4th row

after the first decrease row until 24 (27,
30) sts remain on the needle. Then work
straight in pattern until you have worked
row 8 (16, 24) of the fifth working of the
pattern chart and the front measures
approximately 50 (53, 55)cm from the
cast-on edge.
Shape shoulder: Continuing in pattern,
cast off 12 (13, 14) sts at the beginning of
the next (right-side) row, then work
pattern to end of row. On the next row,
slip one st, then work pattern to end. Cast
off remaining sts.

Right front
Work as for left front, but reverse pocket,
armhole, neck and shoulder shapings.

BACK

With 2¾mm needles and yarn B, cast on
132 (144, 156) sts. Work 5cm in k1, p1
twisted rib in yarn B. Change to 3mm
needles and continue to work entire back
in twisted rib in the following three-colour
stripe sequence:
Row 1: Yarn B
Row 2: Yarn C
Row 3: Yarn A
Carry wools not in use up the sides of the
work until required. Continue repeating
rows 1–3 of stripe pattern until the back
measures the same as the fronts from cast-
on edge to start of armhole shaping,
ending on a wrong-side row – approximately 30 (31, 32)cm.
Shape armholes: Cast off 3 (4, 6) sts at
the beginning of the next and following
row. Then k2 tog at each end of every
row until 100 (104, 108) sts remain on the
needle. Continuing in stripes, work

straight until back measures the same as
the fronts from cast-on edge to start of
shoulder shaping, ending on a wrong-side
row – approximately 50 (53, 55)cm.
Shape shoulders: Continuing in pattern,
cast off 9 (10, 10) sts at the beginning of
the next 2 rows. Then cast off 9 (9, 10) sts
at the beginning of the next 4 rows.
Divide the remaining 44 (48, 50) sts in
half and transfer each half to a spare
needle or stitch holder.

Join fronts to back at shoulders.

FRONT BANDS

Right front
With right side of work facing, and using
2¾mm needles and yarn B, beginning at
lower edge, pick up and knit 97 (101, 105)
sts up front opening edge to start of neck
shaping. Then pick up and knit a further
82 (88, 93) sts around neck to centre-back,
including the 22 (24, 25) sts on the first
spare needle – 179 (189, 198) sts in all.
Work 3 rows in k1, p1 twisted rib in
yarn B.
Buttonholes: Make 5 buttonholes in the
4th row of ribbing as follows: rib 4 sts,
cast off 3 sts, rib 19 (20, 21) sts; repeat
from * 3 more times, cast off 3 sts and rib
to end of row. On the next row, work back
in rib but cast on 3 sts directly over those
cast off in previous row. Work 4 more
rows in rib in yarn B. Join in yarn C and
work one row in rib in yarn C. Cast off in
rib in yarn C.

Left front
Beginning at the centre-back of neck, rib
the 22 (24, 25) sts on the remaining spare

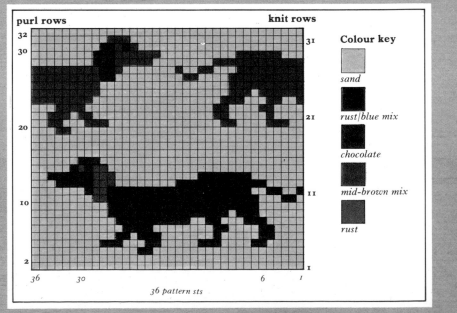

purl rows · knit rows

32 30 · 31 · 20 · 21 · 10 · 11 · 2 · 1

36 · 30 · 6 · 1

36 pattern sts

Colour key

sand
rust/blue mix
chocolate
mid-brown mix
rust

needle and then pick up and knit 60 (64, 68) sts as far as start of neck shaping; then pick up and knit 97 (101, 105) sts down left front to lower edge – 179 (189, 198) sts in all. Work to correspond with right front band but omit buttonholes.

ARMHOLE BANDS

With right side of work facing, and using 2¾mm needles and yarn B, pick up and knit 145 (153, 161) sts around one armhole. Work band to correspond with left front border. Repeat for other armhole.

POCKETS

Pocket tops

With right side facing, using 2¾mm needles and yarn B, pick up and knit 28 (32, 36) sts across the lower cast-off edge of one pocket slit. Work to correspond with left border. Repeat for other pocket.

Pocket linings

Holding work upside down and with right side facing, using 2¾mm needles and yarn B, pick up and knit 28 (32, 36) sts across the upper cast-off edge of one pocket slit, behind pocket top. Work 7cm in st st in yarn B, starting with a purl row. Cast off. Repeat for other pocket.

TO MAKE UP

Press all pieces lightly from the wrong side, avoiding ribbing. Join fronts to back at side seams. Join ribbing at centre-back of neck and underarm points with flat seams. Catch down pocket linings to wrong side of waistcoat fronts and sew down sides of each pocket top. Sew on the five buttons to left front band to correspond with buttonholes.

PROWLING CATS

*Stealthy Ginger Toms and Black Alley Cats
tip-toe across this one-size crew neck baggy sweater.
The neckband, welt and cuffs are all worked in striped rib.*

MATERIALS

Yarn
Use 2-ply jumper weight Shetland yarn.
Yarn A 275g *(oat)*
Yarn B 75g *(black)*
Yarn C 75g *(rust mix)*
Yarn D 25g *(deep pink mix)*
Yarn E 25g *(jade mix)*
Needles
1 pair size 3¼mm
1 pair size 2¾mm
1 set of four size 2¾mm double-pointed
or circular 2¾mm needle

BACK

**With 2¾mm needles and yarn B, cast on
135 sts. Work in k1, p1 twisted rib in the
following two-colour stripe sequence:
Row 1: Yarn B
Row 2: Yarn C
Row 3: Yarn C
Row 4: Yarn B
Repeat rows 1–4 until work measures
approximately 5cm, ending with row 4 of
stripe sequence. On the next row increase
as follows: (yarn B) *p8; purl twice into
the next st; repeat from * to end of row –
150 sts.
Change to 3¼mm needles and st st and
work Fair Isle pattern from chart, reading
odd (knit) rows from right to left, and
even (purl) rows from left to right. Repeat
the 30 pattern sts five times across the row
in all. (You may prefer to darn in the cat's
eyes instead of carrying yarns across.)
Continuing in pattern, work straight until
you have worked row 60 of the second
working of the pattern chart, and the back
measures approximately 45cm from cast-
on edge.
Shape armhole: Cast off 10 sts at the
beginning of the next 2 rows – 130 sts.**
Then work armhole edges straight until
you have worked row 62 of the third
working of the pattern chart, and the back
measures approximately 66cm from cast-
on edge.
Shape shoulders: With right side facing,
continue to work back in st st and yarn A
only. Cast off 15 sts at the beginning of
the next 2 rows. Then cast off 13 sts at the
beginning of the next 4 rows; transfer the
remaining 48 sts to a spare needle or
stitch holder.

FRONT

Work the same as for back from ** to **
(130 sts) so that ribbing, pattern and start
of armhole shaping all match. Then continue to work armhole edges straight until
you have worked row 30 of third working
of pattern chart, and the front measures
approximately 56cm from cast-on edge.
Shape neck: On the next row, work the

purl rows / **knit rows**

Colour key

oat

black

rust mix

deep pink mix

jade mix

30 pattern sts

first 47 sts in the pattern, then slip these
47 sts on to a spare needle or stitch holder.
Cast off the next 36 sts in the row and
then continue to work the last 47 sts of
row in the pattern. Continuing in pattern
on these last 47 sts, decrease one st at the
neck edge on the next 6 rows. Then work
the remaining 41 sts straight, until the
right front measures the same as the back
from cast-on edge to start of shoulder
shaping – approximately 66cm – ending
on row 61 of third working of pattern
chart.
Shape shoulder: (Right shoulder) Cast
off 15 sts at the beginning of the next row
using yarn A, then cast off 13 sts at the
beginning of the following 2 alternate rows.
With the wrong side facing, rejoin the
yarn to the remaining 47 sts on the spare
needle at the left front. Finish left neck
edge and shoulder to correspond with
right neck edge, reversing all shapings.

SLEEVES

With 2¾mm needles and yarn B, cast on
60 sts. Work 9cm in k1, p1 twisted rib,
following same two-colour sequence as for
back welt.
Change to 3¼mm needles and work Fair
Isle pattern from chart as before, repeating the 30 pattern sts twice across rows
and increasing one st at each end of the
3rd and every following 4th row until
there are 130 sts on the needle. Take the
extra sts into the pattern as they are made.
When there are 130 sts on the needle,
work straight in pattern until you have
worked row 6 of the third working of the
pattern chart, and the sleeve measures
approximately 52cm. Cast off right across.
(This cast-off edge across top of sleeve fits
around top of armhole. The last 4cm of
sleeve seam fits across straight cast-off
edge at bottom of armhole.)
Make another sleeve in the same way.

NECKBAND

Join front to back at shoulders. With right side facing, using the four 2¾mm double-pointed needles or the circular needle and yarn B, beginning at the left shoulder, pick up and knit 34 sts down the left side of the neck, 34 sts across the cast-off edge at the centre-front, 34 sts up the right side of the neck as far as shoulder seam, and finally the 48 sts on the spare needle around the back of the neck – 150 sts in all. Work 12 rounds in twisted rib, following the same two-colour sequence as for back welt. Cast off in rib in yarn B.

MEASUREMENTS

One-size; to fit chest 91–99cm (36–39in). (*See also chart on p. 122.*)
Tension
30 sts and 30 rows measure 10cm over Cats pattern on 3¼mm needles.

TO MAKE UP

Press all pieces carefully from the wrong side, avoiding ribbing. Join front to back at sides. Join sleeve seams in the same way, leaving the last 4cm at the top of the seam unstitched. With wrong sides together, pin straight cast-off edge of sleeve head around top of armhole; pin each side of the unstitched section of the sleeve seam across the straight cast-off edge at the bottom of the armhole. Stitch sleeve into armhole. Repeat for other sleeve. Press seams.

ALEXANDER BEETLE

*A buttonless waistcoat worked in Beetle pattern
against a plain background. The front bands, hem, armbands and pocket tops
are all worked from a separate border pattern.*

MATERIALS

Yarn
Use 2-ply jumper weight Shetland yarn.
Yarn A 175g *(oat)*
Yarn B 50g *(peat)*
Yarn C 25g *(crimson)*
Yarn D 25g *(royal blue)*
Yarn E 25g *(emerald green)*
Yarn F 25g *(rust/blue mix)*
Yarn G 25g *(purple)*

Needles
1 pair size 3¼mm
1 pair size 3mm
1 pair size 2¾mm

MEASUREMENTS

To fit chest 86 (91)cm (34, 36in).
(See also chart on p. 123.)

Tension
30 sts and 30 rows measure 10cm over
Beetle pattern on 3¼mm needles.

BACK

Hem: With 2¾mm needles and yarn A,
cast on 132 (144) sts. Work 12 rows in st
st in yarn A, ending with a purl row.

Hem border: Change to 3¼mm needles,
and still in st st, work the 12 rows of the
border pattern from chart A, reading odd
(knit) rows from right to left and even
(purl) rows from left to right. *For the
smaller size (86cm),* repeat sts 1–10,
thirteen times across a knit row and then
work sts 1–2 to finish the row; *for the
larger size (91cm)* work sts 1–10, fourteen
times across the row and then work sts
1–4 to finish the row. Work purl rows in
reverse. Continue in border pattern until
the 12 rows have been completed.

Turn to chart B and work the Beetle
pattern as follows: *for the smaller size
(86cm),* repeat the basic 20 pattern sts (sts
1–20) six times across the row and then
work sts 1–12 to finish the row; *for the
larger size (91cm),* work sts 1–20 seven
times across the row and then work sts
1–4 to finish the row. Work purl rows in
reverse. Continue thus in pattern, until
you have worked row 80 of the first working of pattern chart (row 2 of second
working of pattern chart), and the back
measures approximately 33 (34)cm from
cast-on edge.

Shape armholes: Continuing in pattern,
cast off 3 (4) sts at the beginning of the
next 2 rows. Then k2 tog, at each end of
every row until 96 (104) sts remain. Continuing in pattern work armhole edge
straight until you have worked row 64 (68)
of the second working of the pattern
chart, and the back measures approximately 56 (57)cm from cast-on edge.

Shape shoulders: Cast off 9 (10) sts at
the beginning of the next 6 rows. Divide
the remaining 42 (44) sts equally in half
and transfer each half to a spare needle or
stitch holder.

FRONTS

Left front

Hem: With 2¾mm needles and yarn A,
cast on 66 (72) sts and work 12 rows in st
st in yarn A, ending with a purl row.

Hem border: Change to 3¼mm needles
and work border pattern from chart A in
st st, as before, but *for the smaller size
(86cm),* on knit rows, work sts 1–10, six
times, and then work sts 1–6 to finish
row, and *for the larger size (91cm),*
work sts 1–10, seven times and then
work sts 1–2 once. Work purl
rows in reverse. Continue to
work pattern until the 12 rows
of the border are complete.

Turn to chart B and work Beetle
pattern from chart as follows:
on knit rows, *for the smaller size,*
repeat sts 1–20, three times across the
row and then work sts 1–6 once; *for the
larger size,* work sts 1–20, three times
across the row and then work sts 1–12
once. Work purl rows in reverse. Continue
to work pattern until you have worked
row 20 of the chart.

Pockets: Introduce pockets in the next
row (row 21) as follows: work the first 20
(22) sts of the row in pattern, cast off the
next 26 (28) sts, then continue pattern
across the last 20 (22) sts of row. On row
22, work pattern across the 20 (22) sts at
beginning of row, cast on 26 (28) sts over
those cast off in previous row, then continue in pattern across last 20 (22) sts in
the row.

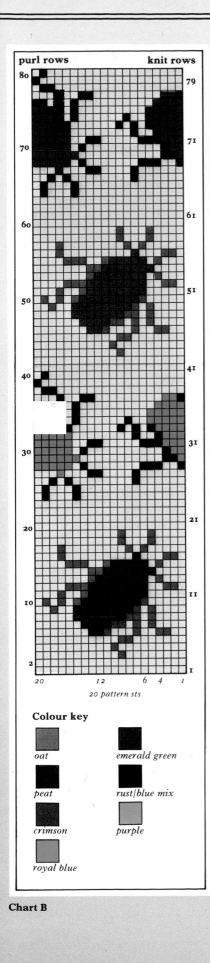

Continuing in pattern, work front straight until you have worked row 80 of first working of pattern chart (row 2 of second working of pattern chart), and front measures same as back from cast-on edge to start of armhole shaping – approximately 33 (34)cm.

Shape armhole and neck edge: Cast off 11 (13) sts at the beginning of the next row, then work pattern to the last 2 sts of row; k2 tog. Continuing in pattern, decrease one st at the armhole edge on the next 15 rows, then work armhole edge straight. *At the same time,* continue to decrease one st on the neck edge on every following 4th row after the first decrease at neck edge, until 26 (27) sts remain on the needle. Then work a few rows straight in pattern, until you have worked row 64 (68) of second working of pattern chart and front measures approximately 56 (57)cm from cast-on edge.

Shape shoulder: Cast off 11 (12) sts at the beginning of the next row – row 65 (69). Slip one st at the beginning of the next row, then continue in pattern to end of row. Cast off.

Right front

Work as for left front, but reverse pocket, armhole, neck and shoulder shapings.

Join fronts to back at shoulders.

BORDERS

Right front

Leave the first 12 rows of plain st st in yarn A free for hem.

With right side facing, using 3mm needles and yarn A, beginning at start of border pattern (row 13), pick up and knit 94 sts up front opening edge as far as start of neck shaping; then continue to pick up and knit 82 (88) sts around neck as far as centre-back, including the 21 (22) sts on the first spare needle – 176 (182) sts in all. Work the next row in purl, using yarn A only. Then work the 12 rows of border pattern from chart A, repeating the 10 pattern sts across the rows, as follows: *for the smaller size* (86cm), work sts *1–10,* seventeen times and then work sts *1–6* once; *for the larger size* (91cm), work sts *1–10,* eighteen times and then work sts *1–2* once. Work purl rows in reverse. When the 12 rows of the pattern are complete, work 12 more rows in st st and yarn A only, starting with a knit row; then cast off in A.

Left front

Beginning at centre-back of neck, in the same way as for right front, knit the 21 (22) sts on the remaining spare needle, then pick up and knit 61 (66) sts around neck to start of neck shaping and then a further 94 sts down front opening edge as far as start of hem border, leaving the 12 rows of st st in yarn A free. Work to correspond with right front border.

Armhole borders

With right side of waistcoat facing, using 3mm needles and yarn A, pick up and knit 134 (140) sts round one armhole. Work the next row in purl in yarn A. Then work border pattern from chart A as follows: *for the smaller size,* on knit rows, repeat sts *1–10,* thirteen times and then work sts *1–4* once; *for the larger size,* work sts *1–10,* fourteen times. Work purl rows in reverse. Continue thus in pattern until the 12 rows are complete. Then change to 2¾mm needles and yarn A and work 12 rows of plain st st in yarn A. Cast off in yarn A. Repeat for other armhole.

POCKETS

Pocket tops

With 2¾mm needles and yarn A, pick up and knit the 24 (26) sts across the lower cast-off edge of one pocket slit. Purl one row in yarn A. Then change to 3mm needles and work border pattern from chart A as follows: *for the smaller size,* work sts *1–10* twice and then *1–4* once; *for the larger size,* work sts *1–10* twice and then *1–6* once. Work purl rows in reverse. Continue in pattern until you have worked row 10 of chart A.
Then change to 2¾mm needles and yarn A and work 8 rows in st st in yarn A only. Cast off. Repeat for other pocket.

Pocket linings

Holding the work upside down and with right side facing, using 2¾mm needles and yarn A, pick up and knit the 26 (28) sts of cast-on edge of one pocket slit behind pocket top. Work 7cm in st st, in yarn A, starting with a purl row. Cast off. Repeat for other pocket.

TO MAKE UP

Press Fair Isle parts lightly from wrong side. Then turn up the 12 rows of plain st st around hem to wrong side. Pin, and slip stitch in position. Join front borders together at centre-back with a flat seam and then turn under plain half of front border in the same way as hem. Pin and slip stitch in position, catching down front border neatly at hem. Join armhole borders at underarm points with flat seams and turn in and slip stitch plain half in the same way. Sew the three free sides of each pocket lining to the back of the waistcoat fronts. Turn in plain half of pocket tops and slip-stitch in position. Then sew down the sides of each pocket top. Press borders lightly.

RAINGIRLS

Rain-girls with umbrellas and boots rush hither and thither across this short cardie which has three-quarter length sleeves, pleated into the armhole.

MATERIALS

Yarn
Use 2-ply jumper weight Shetland yarn.
Yarn A 125g *(oat)*
Yarn B 50g *(red)*
Yarn C 50g *(yellow)*
Yarn D 50g *(black)*
Yarn E 25g *(orange mix)*
Yarn F 25g *(leaf green)*
Yarn G 25g *(bright blue)*

Needles
1 pair size 3¼mm
1 pair size 2¼mm

Notions
5 buttons

MEASUREMENTS

To fit chest 86 (91)cm (34, 36in).

Tension
31 sts and 32 rows measure 10cm over Raingirls pattern on 3¼mm needles.

BACK

With 2¼mm needles and yarn D, cast on 124 (128) sts. Work 5cm in k1, p1 twisted rib in yarn D, increasing across the last (wrong-side) row as follows: rib 2 sts, *rib 9 (8) sts, rib twice into the next st; repeat from * 11 (13) more times, rib 2 sts – 136 (144) sts.

Change to 3¼mm needles and st st and work pattern from chart, reading odd (knit) rows from right to left and even (purl) rows from left to right. Work the pattern across knit rows as follows: *for the smaller size (86cm)*, repeat sts *1–28* four times and then work sts *1–24* once; *for the larger size (91cm)*, repeat sts *1–28* five times and then work sts *1–4* once. Work purl rows in reverse. Join in separate lengths of yarns B, C, G and F when working dolls. Continue thus in pattern, until you have completed row 72 of chart and back measures approximately 28cm.

Shape armholes: Continuing in pattern, cast off 8 sts at the beginning of the next 2 rows. Then k2 tog at each end of every row, 10 times – 100 (108) sts. Work straight in pattern until end of row 62 (66) of the second working of chart and back measures approximately 47 (48)cm.

Shape shoulders: Continuing in pattern, cast off 6 sts at the beginning of the next 4 rows. Then cast off 6 (7) sts at the beginning of the following 6 rows. Divide the remaining 40 (42) sts in half and leave each half on a spare needle or stitch holder.

FRONTS

Left front

With 2¼mm needles and yarn D, cast on 56 (58) sts. Work 5cm in k1, p1 twisted rib, increasing across last (wrong-side) row as follows: rib one st, *rib 8 (6) sts, rib twice into the next st; repeat from * 5 (7) times more, rib one st – 62 (66) sts. Change to 3¼mm needles and st st and work pattern from chart. Work pattern across knit rows as follows: *for the smaller size*, repeat sts *1–28* twice and then work sts *1–6* once; *for the larger size,* repeat sts *1–28* twice and then work sts *1–10* once. Work purl rows in reverse. Continue in pattern until you have completed row 64 of the pattern chart and front measures approximately 25cm.

Shape neck and armhole: Continuing in pattern, *work pattern across the next (right-side) row to last 2 sts; k2 tog. Work 3 rows straight*. Repeat from * to * once more – 60 (64) sts. Continue to shape neck, decreasing one st at the neck edge on every following 5th row after first decrease and *at the same time*, shape armhole by casting off 8 sts at the beginning of the next row (row 1 of second working of chart). Then k2 tog at armhole edge on the following 10 rows. Then work armhole edge straight but continue to decrease at front edge on every 5th row, as before, until 30 (33) sts remain. Now work straight in pattern until you have completed row 62 (66) of the second working of chart and front measures approximately 47 (48)cm.

Shape shoulders: Cast off 6 sts at the beginning of the next and following alternate row; then cast off 6 (7) sts at the beginning of the following 3 alternate rows.

Right front

Work as for left front, but reverse neck, armhole and shoulder shapings.

SLEEVES

With 2¼mm needles and yarn D, cast on 64 sts. Work 7cm in k1, p1 twisted rib, increasing across the last (wrong-side) row as follows: rib 10 sts, rib twice into each of the next 44 sts, rib 10 sts – 108 sts. Change to 3¼mm needles and st st and work pattern from chart. Work pattern across knit rows as follows: *for both sizes,* repeat sts *1–28* three times and then work sts *1–24* once to complete row. Work purl rows in reverse. Continue in pattern until you have completed row 72 of the first working of chart and sleeve measures approximately 29cm from cast-on edge.

Shape top of sleeve: Continuing in pattern, cast off 8 sts at the beginning of the next 2 rows. Then k2 tog at each end of the next and every following alternate row, 10 times – 72 sts. Now work 20 (24) rows straight in pattern, then k2 tog at each end of the next and every following alternate row, 6 times in all – 60 sts. Then k2 tog at end of the following 10 rows – 40 sts. Cast off – this wide sleeve top will be pleated into the armhole later.

Join both shoulder seams.

FRONT BANDS

Right front

With 2¼mm needles and yarn D, beginning at the lower edge and with right side facing, pick up and knit 93 sts up front opening edge to start of neck shaping; then pick up and knit a further 99 (103) sts around neck to centre-back including the 20 (21) sts on the first spare needle at the back of neck – 192 (196) sts. Work 3 rows in k1, p1 twisted rib.

Buttonholes: Make 5 buttonholes in 4th row as follows: rib 4 sts, *cast off 3 sts, rib 18 sts; repeat from * three more times, cast off 3 sts, rib to end. Rib back along 5th row, casting on 3 sts over those cast off in the previous row. Work a further 3 rows in rib. Cast off.

Left front

Work in the same way as right front, but begin picking up sts at the centre-back of neck with the 20 (21) sts on remaining spare needle and work to lower edge, and omit buttonholes.

TO MAKE UP

Press all pieces lightly from wrong side, avoiding ribbing. Join ribbing, side seams and sleeve seams. Pin sleeve into armhole, pleating the fullness around the top of the sleeve into 3 pleats to fit armhole either side of shoulder seam. Sew in position and repeat for other sleeve. Press seams from wrong side. Sew buttons on to left front band to correspond with buttonholes.

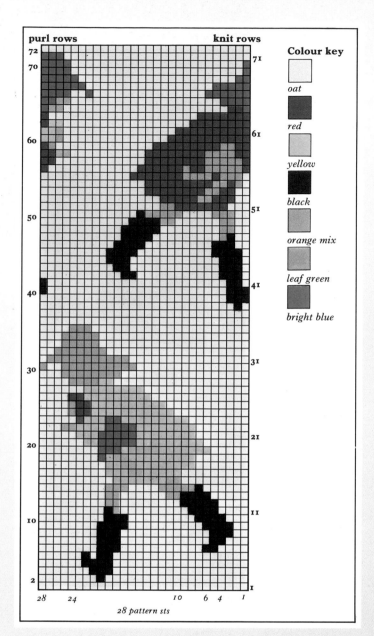

purl rows — knit rows

72 70 60 50 40 30 20 10 2
71 61 51 41 31 21 11 1

28 24 10 6 4 1

28 pattern sts

Colour key

oat

red

yellow

black

orange mix

leaf green

bright blue

COTTON CATS

*Cats gazing out of windows on summer days set against a background
of pale grey and yellow stripes form the pattern for this cotton waistcoat.
The back of the waistcoat is worked in striped rib.*

MATERIALS

Yarn
Use No. 8 cotton yarn.
Yarn A 250g *(pale grey)*
Yarn B 150g *(écru)*
Yarn C 50g *(deep pink)*
Yarn D 50g *(bluebell)*
Yarn E 50g *(brown)*
Yarn F 50g *(black)*

Needles
1 pair size 3¼mm
1 pair size 3mm
1 pair size 2¾mm

Notions
5 × 1.5cm buttons

MEASUREMENTS

To fit chest 84 (91, 99)cm (33, 36, 39in).
(See also chart on p. 123.)

Tension
32 sts and 32 rows measure 10cm over
Cotton Cats pattern on 3¼mm needles.

FRONTS

Left front
With 2¾mm needles and yarn A, cast on
64 (70, 76) sts. Work 5cm in k1, p1
twisted rib in yarn A, increasing one st at
each end of the final (wrong-side) row – 66
(72, 78) sts.
Change to 3¼mm needles and st st and
work pattern from chart reading odd
(knit) rows from right to left and even
(purl) rows from left to right. Work the
pattern across knit rows as follows: *for the
small size* (84cm), work sts *15–20* at the
beginning of row and then repeat sts *1–20*
three times; *for the medium size* (91cm),
work sts *9–20* once, and then repeat sts
1–20 three times; *for the large size* (99cm),
work sts *3–20* once and then repeat sts
1–20 three times. Work purl rows in
reverse. Continue in pattern until you have
completed row 22 of chart.

Pocket:
Introduce pocket in row 23 of
pattern chart as follows: work the first 19
(20, 21) sts of the row, then cast off the
next 28 (32, 36) sts, and continue in
pattern across the last 19 (20, 21) sts in the
row. On the next row (row 24), work the
first 19 (20, 21) sts in the row, then cast
on 28 (32, 36) sts directly over those
cast off in previous row, and continue in
pattern across the last 19 (20, 21) sts in the
row. Continuing in pattern, work straight
until you have completed row 26 (30, 34)
of the second working of the pattern chart
and front measures
approximately
29 (30, 31)cm
from cast-on edge.

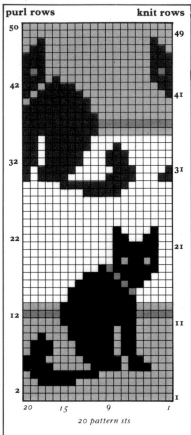

purl rows — *knit rows*

50 — 49

42 — 41

32 — 31

22 — 21

12 — 11

2 — 1

20   15   9   1
20 pattern sts

Colour key

pale grey	*bluebell*
écru	*brown*
deep pink	*black*

Shape armhole and neck:
Cast off 8
(10, 12) sts at the beginning of the next
row, then work pattern to the last 2 sts,
k2 tog. Continuing in pattern, decrease
one st at the armhole edge on the next 17
rows; then work armhole edge straight. *At
the same time,* continue to decrease one st
at the neck edge on every following 4th
row after the first decrease on row 27 of
chart, until 26 (28, 30) sts remain. Then
work neck edge straight until front
measures approximately 52 (55, 57)cm.

(When you have completed the third
working of the pattern chart, work the
few extra rows needed in yarn A, to avoid
having fragments of pattern at the
shoulder edge.)

Shape shoulder:
Using yarn A, cast off
10 sts at the beginning of the next (right-
side) row. Then cast off 8 (9, 10) sts at the
beginning of the following 2 alternate
rows.

Right front
Work as for left front, but reverse pocket,
armhole, neck and shoulder shapings.

BACK

With 2¾mm needles and yarn A,
cast on 128 (140, 152) sts. Work
5cm in k1, p1 twisted rib in yarn A,
increasing 4 sts across the last
(wrong-side) row by working
twice into every 32nd
(35th, 38th) st, four
times in all –
132 (144, 152)
sts.

Change to 3mm needles
and continue to work entire
back in k1, p1 twisted rib in the
following three-colour stripe sequence:
Row 1: Yarn B
Row 2: Yarn D
Row 3: Yarn A
Work straight, repeating rows 1–3 until
the back measures the same as the fronts

from cast-on edge to start of armhole shaping – approximately 29 (30, 31)cm.

Shape armholes: Cast off 3 (4, 6) sts at the beginning of the next 2 rows. Then k2 tog at each end of every row until 100 (104, 110) sts remain. Work straight until the back measures the same as the fronts from cast-on edge to start of shoulder shaping – approximately 52 (55, 57)cm.

Shape shoulders: On the next right-side row, cast off 9 (10, 10) sts at the beginning of this and the following row. Then cast off 9 (9, 10) sts at the beginning of the following 4 rows. Divide the remaining 46 (48, 50) sts equally in half and transfer each half to a spare needle or stitch holder.

Join fronts to back at shoulders.

FRONT BANDS

Right front
With 2¾mm needles and yarn A and beginning at the lower edge, pick up and knit 97 (101, 105) sts up right front opening edge as far as start of neck shaping; then continue to pick up and knit a further 80 (84, 88) sts around the neck edge as far as the centre-back, including the 23 (24, 25) sts on the first spare needle. Work 3 rows of k1, p1 twisted rib in yarn A.

Buttonholes: Make 5 buttonholes in 4th row of ribbing as follows: rib 4 sts, *cast off 3 sts, rib 19 (20, 21) sts; repeat from * three more times, then cast off 3 sts and rib to end of row. On the next row (row 5) work back in rib, but cast on 3 sts directly over those cast off in previous row. Work 4 more rows in rib in yarn A. Join in yarn D and work one row in twisted rib in yarn D. Cast off in rib in yarn D.

Left front
Beginning at centre-back, with yarn A and 2¾mm needles, rib the first 23 (24, 25) sts from the spare needle; then pick up and knit the remaining 57 (60, 63) sts as far as the start of the neck shaping; then continue to pick up and knit 97 (101, 105) sts down front to lower edge. Work to correspond with right front band, but omit buttonholes.

ARMHOLE BANDS

With the right side facing, using 2¾mm needles and yarn A, pick up and knit 145 (153, 161) sts around one armhole. Then work 10 rows in k1, p1 twisted rib in yarn A. Join in yarn D and work a further row of rib. Cast off in rib in yarn D. Repeat for other armhole.

POCKETS

Pocket tops
With the right side of waistcoat front facing, using 2¾mm needles and yarn A, pick up and knit the 28 (32, 36) sts across the lower cast-off edge of one pocket slit. Work 11 rows of k1, p1 twisted rib to correspond with left front border. Repeat for other pocket opening.

Pocket linings
Holding waistcoat upside down, and with the right side facing, using 3mm needles and yarn A, pick up and knit the 28 (32, 36) sts across the cast-on edge of one pocket slit, behind pocket top. Starting with a purl row, work 7cm in st st in yarn A; then cast off. Repeat for other pocket.

TO MAKE UP

Press fronts and back lightly from wrong side, avoiding all ribbing. Join front to back at side seams. Join ribbing at centre-back and underarm points with flat seams. Sew the three free sides of each pocket lining to the wrong side of the waistcoat fronts. Sew down each side of the pocket tops. Sew the 5 buttons to the left front border to correspond with buttonholes.

WINTER SCOTTIES

*Black and white Scotty dogs worked in Shetland yarn
in a variety of garments for men and women.*

WINTER SCOTTIES

Chart A

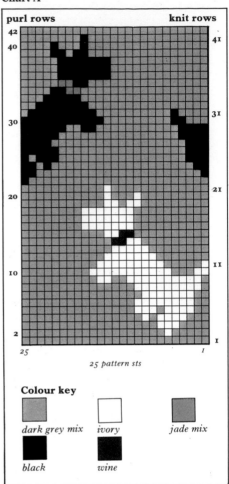

purl rows   knit rows

42 40   41
30   31
20   21
10   11
2   1
25   1

25 pattern sts

Colour key

dark grey mix   ivory   jade mix

black   wine

MATERIALS Hat

Yarn
Use 2-ply jumper weight Shetland yarn.
Yarn A 50g (*dark grey mix*)
Yarn B 25g (*black*)
Yarn C 25g (*ivory*)
Yarn D 25g (*wine*)
Yarn E 25g (*jade mix*)
Needles
Set of four size 3¼mm *or*
circular size 3¼mm
Set of four size 2¾mm *or*
circular size 2¾mm

MEASUREMENTS

One-size: to fit an average head.
(*See also chart on p. 123.*)
Tension
32 sts and 32 rows measure 10cm over
Scotty pattern on 3¼mm needles.

Headband
Work in the round. With 2¾mm needles
and yarn B, cast on 160 sts (53 sts on each
of two needles and 54 on the third needle
if using four needles). Work 11cm in k1,
p1 twisted rib in the following three-
colour stripe sequence:

Round 1: Yarn A
Round 2: Yarn D
Round 3: Yarn B
Repeat rounds 1–3, ending with a round
in yarn B. Join in yarn A and increase
across the next row as follows: knit 35 sts,
knit twice into each of the next 90 sts,
knit 35 sts – 250 sts.
Change to 3¼mm needles and work Scotty
pattern from chart, working in rounds,
reading *every* row knit on chart A
from right to left. Repeat sts *1–25* ten
times across one round. Work in pattern
until you have completed row 21 of the
second working of the pattern chart.
Shape crown: Change from pattern back
to the three-colour stripe sequence as
before (yarn A, yarn D, yarn B) and
decrease as follows:
Round 1: (Yarn A) *k8, slip 1, k1, psso;
repeat from * all round.
Work 2 rounds straight (yarns D and B).
Round 4: (Yarn A) *k7, slip 1, k1, psso,
repeat from * all round (200 sts).
Work 2 rounds straight (yarns D and B).
Round 7: (Yarn A) *k6, slip 1, k1, psso,
repeat from * all round (175 sts).
Continue to decrease in this way on every
third round until you have worked the
round *k2, slip 1, k1, psso; repeat from *
to end (50 sts). On the next round, k2 tog
all round – 25 sts. Work 2 rounds straight.
Repeat these last 3 rounds twice more.
Break yarn, leaving about a 15cm end.
Thread the end through the remaining
sts, draw up and secure.

TO MAKE UP

Press lightly from wrong side, avoiding
ribbing. Fold ribbed headband in half to
inside and pin in position. Slip stitch this
inner edge loosely to inside of hat so that
stitches will stretch when the hat is put on.

MATERIALS Legwarmers

Yarn
Use 2-ply jumper weight Shetland yarn.
Yarn A 100g (*dark grey mix*)
Yarn B 75g (*black*)
Yarn C 50g (*ivory*)
Yarn D 25g (*wine*)
Yarn E 25g (*jade mix*)
Needles
1 pair size 3¼mm
1 pair size 2¾mm
Notions
1½mm of fine hat elastic.

MEASUREMENTS

One-size: to fit an average leg.
(*See also chart on p. 123.*)
Tension
32 sts and 32 rows measure 10cm over
Scotty pattern on 3¼mm needles.

Lower welt
With 2¾mm needles and yarn B, cast on
125 sts. Work 10cm in k1, p1 twisted rib.
Join in yarn D and work 2 rows in yarn D
in rib.
Change to 3¼mm needles and st st and
work Scotty pattern from chart, reading
odd (knit) rows from right to left and even
(purl) rows from left to right. Repeat the
25 pattern sts (*1–25*) five times across the
rows. Work straight in pattern until you
have completed row 42 of the second
working of the pattern chart. (For longer
legwarmers, work the 42 rows of the
pattern again.) Join in yarn D and work 2
rows in twisted rib in yarn D. Then join
in yarn B and work 10cm in twisted rib.
Cast off in rib in yarn D. Make another
legwarmer in the same way.

TO MAKE UP

Press both pieces lightly from the wrong
side, avoiding ribbing. Join back seam of
each legwarmer. Cut lengths of elastic to
fit around lower and upper edges of legwarmers and thread through the cast-on
and cast-off edges of the welts from the
wrong side, securing ends. For wider
legwarmers, do not apply the elastic to
the lower edge.

Chart B

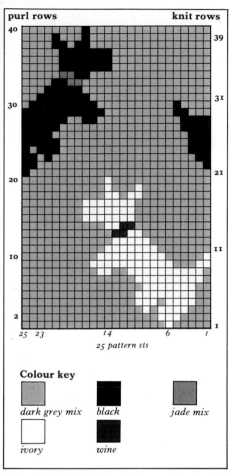

purl rows   **knit rows**

25 pattern sts

Colour key

dark grey mix	black	jade mix
ivory	wine	

MATERIALS Jumper

Yarn

Use 2-ply jumper weight Shetland yarn.
Different sizes will require different
quantities of main yarn.
Yarn A 225 (250, 250, 250)g *(dark grey mix)*
Yarn B 100g *(ivory)*
Yarn C 75g *(black)*
Yarn D 25g *(wine)*
Yarn E 25g *(jade mix)*

Needles

1 pair size 3¼mm
1 pair size 2¾mm
1 pair size 2¼mm
1 set of four double pointed size 2¾mm

MEASUREMENTS

To fit chest 91 (96, 102, 106)cm (36, 38,
40, 42in).
(See also chart on p. 123.)

Tension

32 sts and 32 rows measure 10cm over
Scotty pattern on 3¼mm needles.

BACK

**With 2¼ (2¼, 2¾, 2¾)mm needles and
yarn B, cast on 132 (136, 144, 152) sts.
Work 5cm in k1, p1 twisted rib increasing
across the last (wrong-side) row as follows:

rib 2 (8, 2, 6) sts, *rib 7 (5, 6, 6) sts, rib
twice into the next st; repeat from * 15
(19, 19, 19) times more, rib 2 (8, 2, 6) sts –
148 (156, 164, 172) sts.
Change to 3¼mm needles and st st and
work Scotty pattern from chart B, reading
odd (knit) rows from right to left and even
(purl) rows from left to right. Work the
pattern across knit rows as follows: *for
size 91cm,* repeat sts *1–25* five times and
work sts *1–23* once to complete row; *for
size 96cm,* repeat sts *1–25* six times and
then work sts *1–6* once; *for size 102cm,*
work sts *1–25* six times and then work sts
1–14 once; *for size 106cm,* work sts *1–25*
six times, and then work sts *1–22* once.
Work purl rows in reverse. Continue thus
in pattern until you have worked row 2
(6, 10, 14) of the fourth working of the
pattern chart and back measures approximately 43 (44, 45, 48)cm from cast-on edge.
Shape armholes: Continuing in pattern,
cast off 12 (12, 14, 16) sts at the beginning
of the next 2 rows.** Then work straight
in pattern until you have completed row
28 (36, 4, 12) of the fifth (fifth, sixth,
sixth) working of the pattern chart and
back measures approximately 63 (66, 70,
71)cm from cast-on edge.
Shape shoulder: Continuing in pattern,
cast off 14 (16, 17, 16) sts at the beginning
of the next 2 rows. Then cast off 13 (13,
13, 14) sts at the beginning of the next 4
rows. Leave the remaining 44 (48, 50, 52)
sts on a spare needle or stitch holder.

FRONT

Work in the same way as back from ** to
** – 124 (132, 136, 140) sts.
Shape neck: Divide for 'V' neck as
follows: on the next row, with right side
facing, work the pattern across the first
60 (64, 66, 68) sts of the row, k2 tog and
turn; leave remaining sts on a spare
needle. Continue in pattern on these first
sts, decreasing one st at the neck edge on
the next and every following 3rd row at
the neck edge, until 40 (42, 43, 44) sts
remain. Then work a few rows straight in
pattern until you have completed row 28
(36, 4, 12) of the fifth (fifth, sixth, sixth)
working of the pattern chart and sleeve
measures approximately 63 (66, 70, 71)cm
from cast-on edge.
Shape shoulder: Continuing in pattern,
cast off 14 (16, 17, 16) sts at the beginning
of the next row, then cast off 13 (13, 13,
14) sts at the beginning of the following 2
alternate rows. Rejoin yarn to remaining
64 (66, 68, 70) sts at the neck edge; k2
tog and work pattern to end of row.
Finish left side of neck and shoulder to
correspond with right side, reversing
shapings.

SLEEVES

With 2¾mm needles and yarn B, cast on
56 (60, 64, 70) sts. Work 9cm in k1, p1
twisted rib, increasing across the last
(wrong-side) row as follows: *rib 6 (4, 7,
13) sts, rib twice into the next st; repeat

from * 7 (11, 7, 4) more times – 64 (72, 72,
75) sts in all.
Change to 3¼mm needles and st st and
work pattern from chart. Work the pattern
across knit rows as follows: *for size 91cm,*
repeat sts *1–25* twice and then work sts
1–14 once; *for sizes 96 and 102cm,* repeat
sts *1–25* twice and then work sts *1–22*
once; *for size 106cm,* work sts *1–25* three
times. Work purl rows in reverse.
Continue in pattern, *at the same time*
shaping the side edges by increasing one
st at each end of the 5th (7th, 5th, 3rd)
row and every following fourth row until
there are 132 (136, 140, 147) sts on the
needle. Take the extra sts into the pattern
as they are made. Now work a few rows
straight in pattern until you have completed row 24 (28, 32, 32) of the fourth
working of the pattern chart and sleeve
measures approximately 54 (55, 56, 56)cm
from cast-on edge. Cast off right across
row – this cast-off should measure
approximately 41 (43, 46, 48)cm to fit
armhole.

NECKBAND

Join both shoulder seams. With the set of
four double pointed size 2¾mm needles
and yarn B, beginning at the left shoulder
seam, pick up and knit 60 (64, 68, 72) sts
down left side of neck edge, knit one st
from the centre, pick up and knit 59 (63,
67, 71) sts up right side of neck, and then
knit the 44 (48, 50, 52) sts from the back
of the neck on spare needle – 164 (176,
186, 196) sts in all. Work 11 rounds of k1,
p1 twisted rib, decreasing one st at each
side of the centre-front st on every round.
Join in yarn D and rib one round,
decreasing as before. Cast off in rib in
yarn D, taking 2 sts together each side of
centre-front as before.

TO MAKE UP

Press all pieces lightly from wrong side,
avoiding ribbing. Join side seams. Join
underarm sleeve seams, leaving 4 (4, 5,
5)cm unstitched at the top of the seam.
Pin straight cast-off edge of top of sleeve
into top of armhole and pin either side of
the unstitched section of the sleeve seam
across the straight cast-off edge at base of
armhole. Sew sleeve in place and repeat
for other sleeve. Press seams lightly from
wrong side.

WINTER SCOTTIES

MATERIALS Waistcoat

Yarn
Use 2-ply jumper weight Shetland yarn.
Yarn A 125g *(pale grey mix)*
Yarn B 125g *(white)*
Yarn C 50g *(black)*
Yarn D 25g *(wine)*
Yarn E 25g *(jade mix)*

Needles
1 pair size 3¾mm
1 pair size 3¼mm
1 pair size 2¾mm
1 cable needle

Notions
4 buttons

MEASUREMENTS

One-size: to fit chest 91–97cm (36–38in).
(See also chart on p. 123.)

Tension
32 sts and 32 rows measure 10cm over
Scotties pattern on 3¼mm needles.

BACK

With 2¾mm needles and yarn B, cast on
140 sts. Work 10cm in k1, p1 twisted rib
in yarn B. Change to yarn A and increase
across the next row as follows: *p6, purl
twice into the next st; repeat from * to end
of row – 160 sts.
Change to 3¼mm needles and st st and
work Scotty pattern from chart, reading
odd (knit) rows from right to left and even
(purl) rows from left to right. Work knit
rows as follows: work sts *1–3* once, then
work sts *4–28*, six times and finally work
sts *4–10* once to complete row. Work purl
rows in reverse. Continue thus, repeating
the 40 rows of the pattern, until you have
worked row 40 of the fourth working of
the pattern chart and back measures
approximately 60cm from the cast-on
edge. Then cast off right across the row.

FRONTS

Left front
**With 2¾mm needles and yarn B, cast on
60 sts. Work 10cm in k1, p1 twisted rib.
Change to yarn A and increase across next
(wrong-side) row as follows: *p4, purl
twice into the next st; repeat from * to
end of row – 72 sts.**
Change to 3¼mm needles and st st and
work pattern from chart, working knit
rows as follows: work sts *11–28* once, then
sts *4–28* twice and finally sts *28–32* once.
Work purl rows in reverse. Continue thus,
repeating the 40 rows of the pattern chart
until you have worked row 22 of the
second working of the pattern chart and
front measures approx. 29cm from cast-on
edge. There are no armhole shapings.
Shape neck: Decrease one st at the neck
edge on the next row (row 23) and every
following 3rd row, 32 times in all – 40 sts.
Then work straight in pattern until you
have worked row 40 of the fourth working
of the pattern chart and front measures
approximately 60cm from cast-on edge.
Cast off right across the row.

Right front
Work right front in the same way as left
front from ** to ** – 72 sts.
Change to 3¼mm needles and st st and
work pattern from chart as for left front,
but reversing all shapings.

CABLE BORDERS

Fronts
Note: To work the instruction 'cable 6'
(see below) work as follows: slip the next
3 sts on to a cable needle and hold to front
of work, knit 3 sts, then knit 3 sts from
cable needle (see also p. 133).
Sew fronts to back at shoulder seams.
With 3¾mm needles and yarn B, cast on
12 sts, then work cable borders as follows:
Row 1: Knit
Row 2: K3, p6, k3
Row 3: Knit
Row 4: K3, p6, k3
Row 5: Knit
Row 6: K3, p6, k3
Row 7: K3, cable 6, k3
Row 8: K3, p6, k3
Row 9: Knit
Row 10: K3, p6, k3
These 10 rows form the cable pattern.
Repeat the first 4 rows (rows 1–4) again.
Buttonholes: Make the first buttonhole in
rows 5 and 6 as follows: *(row 5) k5 sts,
cast off 2 sts, k5 sts. On the next row (row
6), k3 sts, p2 sts, cast on 2 sts, p2 sts, k3
sts. Then work the next 28 rows in cable
pattern (rows 7–10, 1–10, 1–10, 1–4).*
Repeat from * to * twice more. Then
make the fourth buttonhole in the next 2
rows (rows 5 and 6 of the 11th working of
the cable pattern). Then continue straight
in cable pattern from row 7 until strip is
long enough to fit up right front opening
edge, around back of neck and back down

left front opening edge, when slightly
stretched. Cast off.

Armholes
With 3¾mm needles and yarn B, cast on
12 sts. Work rows 1–10 of cable pattern as
for front border, repeating them until
strip measures 51cm. Cast off. Repeat for
other armhole.

TO MAKE UP

Press all pieces lightly from wrong side,
including cable borders, but avoiding
ribbing. Join side seams starting at a point
10cm down from shoulder edge to allow
for armhole, and sewing down to lower
edge, so forming the armholes. Pin front
cable border in position around front
opening edges – the top buttonhole should
come just below the start of the neck
shaping on the right front opening edge.
Sew cable border to main work with a flat
seam sewn from the wrong side.
Armhole borders: Join the short ends of
one armhole border by placing one end
over the other so that the wrong side of
the top end is against the right side of the
underneath end and the two ends form a
'V' (see p. 140). Pin into armhole so that
the point of the 'V' fits into the bottom of
the armhole. Sew into armhole as before.
Repeat for other armhole. Sew on buttons
to left front border to match buttonholes.

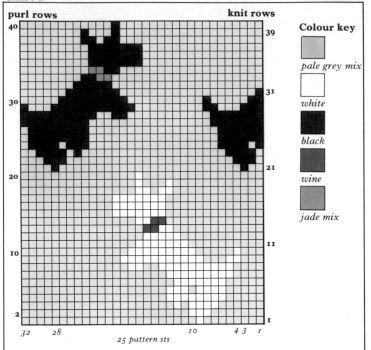

Chart C

purl rows   knit rows

Colour key

pale grey mix

white

black

wine

jade mix

25 pattern sts

MEASUREMENTS
AND YARNS

GEOMETRIC

Alongside the measurements charts on the following pages are samples of the yarns used in each of the individual sweaters. Whereas the coloured boxes given with the pattern charts are representative of the shades used, the yarns given below are the exact colours found in each sweater. Different yarns such as cotton or mohair are not distinguished here – see the patterns for these details.

DESERT RIBBONS p. 24
A 46cm bust
B 51cm length
C 31cm sleeve

sand
ivory
pale lilac mix
mid-brown mix
pearl
sage green

HARRIET p. 20
A 52 (54)cm bust
B 86 (87)cm length
C 54 (54)cm sleeve

dark fawn
blue/wine mix
peat
pale lilac mix
rust
pale green mix
lilac/green mix
rust/blue mix
pale pink mix
rust mix

OPTICAL COPPER p. 26
A 43 (47, 50)cm chest
B 52 (54, 56)cm length

black
copper
rust
peat
wine

Hat 33cm from crown to edge of headband

PAINTBOX p. 22
A 42 (46, 51)cm chest
B 58 (61, 63)cm length

white
yellow
brown
pale green
pink
rust
mid-blue
bottle green
lilac

RIBS p. 28
A 34cm bust
B 54cm length
C 50cm sleeve

deep pink mix

BRAMBLE p. 28

A 45cm bust
B 54cm length
C 46cm sleeve

petrol blue

SQUARES ON BLACK p. 36

A 60 (62, 67)cm length
B 43 (46, 49)cm bust
C 39 (43, 44)cm sleeve

black
yellow
peat
sage green
pink
rust
ivory
green
lilac/green mix
bluebell

RIBBONS p. 32

A 46 (49)cm chest
B 61 (62)cm length
C 49 (51)cm sleeve

peat
black
red
green
bright blue
mustard

Hat 88cm from bobble to edge of headband

COPPER DIAMONDS p. 38

A 44 (48, 52, 56)cm chest
B 62 (65, 68, 71)cm length
C 49 (49, 49, 49)cm sleeve

blue/orange mix
blue/fawn mix
mid-blue mix
copper
mid-brown mix
oat
bright blue
rust/blue mix
tan

CHEQUER-BOARD p. 34

A 48 (54)cm chest
B 70 (72)cm length
C 51 (53)cm sleeve

oat
ivory
dark fawn
rust
lilac/green mix
clan green
bottle green
purple
peat

MAURICE p. 40

A 47 (50, 53)cm chest
B 53 (57, 59)cm length

blue/wine mix
peat
lilac/green mix
pale green mix
rust mix
rust/blue mix
pale lilac mix
rust
dark fawn
pale pink mix

FLOWERS

WALLFLOWERS p. 44
A 46 (49)cm bust
B 57 (59)cm length
C 45 (45)cm sleeve

écru
beige
orange
crimson
olive
yellow

A
B
C

PURPLE PANSY p. 50
A 49cm chest
B 72cm length
C 54cm sleeve

ivory
purple
oat
yellow
clan green
pale lilac mix
wine
violet
bluebell
navy
wine mix
silver

A
B
C

IRIS p. 46
A 44 (47)cm bust
B 54 (55)cm length
C 45 (46)cm sleeve

pale lilac mix
lilac/green mix
violet
purple
sage green
wine
pale yellow
yellow
gold
wine mix

A
B
C

ROSES p. 52
A 45 (47)cm bust
B 59 (61)cm length
C 49 (49)cm sleeve

écru
pale grey
pale blue
mid-blue
brown
pink
deep pink

A
B
C

MARIGOLD p. 48
A 44 (46, 50)cm bust
B 54 (56, 59)cm length

brown/green mix
rust
yellow
dark orange mix
copper
chocolate
clan green
brown mix

A
B

DAISY p. 54
A 43 (47, 50)cm chest
B 52 (54, 55)cm length

pale grey mix
ivory
yellow
dark grey mix
peat
sage green
silver
pale grey

A
B

Hat 30cm from crown to edge of headband

ETHNIC

SWEET PEAS p. 56

A 38 (39)cm bust
B 37 (38)cm length

écru
purple
bluebell
pale green
pink
deep pink
beige

PRETTY PANSIES p. 58

A 46cm bust
B 53cm length
C 31cm sleeve

ivory
pale yellow
pale lilac mix
powder blue
wine mix
lilac/green mix
clan green
pale pink mix
white
silver

CACTUS p. 62

A 45 (49, 53, 56)cm chest
B 58 (61, 63, 66)cm length

clan green
bottle green
peat
pale green mix
dark fawn
oat
pale grey mix
mustard
blue/wine mix
red/blue mix

DOUBLE DUTCH p. 64

A 52cm chest
B 67cm length
C 52cm sleeve

navy
ivory
crimson

NAVAJO p. 66

A 43 (47, 50)cm chest
B 57 (59, 62)cm length

oat
rust
black
mustard
lilac/green mix
olive mix

PIERROT p. 68
A 44 (47)cm chest
B 52 (54)cm length
C 44 (46)cm sleeve

écru
pale blue
lilac
bluebell
deep pink
yellow
purple

CHITIMACHA p. 74
A 45 (53)cm chest
B 49 (58)cm length

rust
mustard
jade mix
oat
black

STERLING ZIG-ZAG p. 70
A 44 (46, 48)cm bust
B 62 (66, 69)cm length
C 43 (44, 45)cm sleeve

wine
olive
mustard
copper
pale lilac mix
fawn
peat
chocolate
dark wine mix

WILLOW p. 76
A 46 (50)cm chest
B 53 (55)cm length

mid-blue mix
ivory
navy

CAMISOLE p. 71
A 33cm bust
B 29cm length of back

peat
wine
copper

ISLAMIC p. 78
A 43 (47, 50)cm chest
B 53 (55, 58)cm length

chocolate
peat
wine
powder blue
ivory
orange mix
blue/orange mix
lilac/green mix
royal blue

LEAVES p. 80
A 43 (46)cm bust
B 55 (58)cm length
C 46 (47)cm sleeve

bottle green

dark fawn

chocolate

rust

peat

brown/green mix

wine

oat

deep pink mix

rust mix

mustard

pale green mix

SUMMER SCOTTY p. 86
A 45 (48)cm bust
B 50 (51)cm length
C 30 (30)cm sleeve

grey

black

white

yellow

lilac

MOSAIC p. 82
A 46 (52, 57)cm chest
B 60 (63, 66)cm length

navy

rust

olive

bottle green

ivory

mustard mix

dark fawn

sage green

rust mix

BOYS ON BLUE p. 88
A 47 (49)cm chest
B 58 (60)cm length
C 51 (51)cm sleeve

pale blue mix

oat

black

red

green

mid-blue

yellow

rust

royal blue

TEDDY-BEAR p. 90
A 47 (50)cm chest
B 56 (58)cm length

dark fawn

chocolate

red

violet

mid-brown

jade mix

mid-blue

SEAGULLS p. 92
A 46 (49, 55)cm chest
B 59 (59, 69)cm length
C 47 (47, 47)cm sleeve

light blue mix

white

light brown

red

black

BUTTERFLIES p. 98
A 49cm chest
B 61cm length

olive mix

light brown

mustard

light blue

bright blue

orange mix

chocolate

oat

STARING CATS p. 94
A 44 (47, 50, 53)cm chest
B 65 (68, 69, 70)cm length
C 48 (48, 50, 50)cm sleeve

red/blue mix

mid-blue mix

ivory

black

rust

yellow

DACHSHUND p. 100
A 42 (47, 50)cm chest
B 52 (55, 57)cm length

sand

mid-brown mix

chocolate

rust/blue mix

rust

BOYS ON BLACK p. 96
A 50 (58)cm chest
B 66 (69)cm length
C 49 (48)cm sleeve

black

bluebell

rust

yellow

red

leaf green

sand

PROWLING CATS p. 102
A 50cm chest
B 68cm length
C 48cm sleeve

oat

black

rust mix

deep pink mix

jade mix

ALEXANDER BEETLE p. 104
A 45 (48)cm chest
B 58 (59)cm length

oat

peat

crimson

royal blue

emerald green

rust/blue mix

purple

WINTER SCOTTIES p. 110
LEGWARMERS AND HAT
A 37cm length

35cm crown to edge of headband

dark grey mix

black

ivory

wine

jade mix

RAINGIRLS p. 106
A 44 (46)cm bust
B 50 (51)cm length
C 29 (29)cm sleeve

oat

red

yellow

black

orange mix

leaf green

bright blue

V-NECK SWEATER
A 46 (49, 51, 54)cm chest
B 65 (68, 72, 73)cm length
C 50 (51, 51, 51)cm sleeve

dark grey mix

ivory

black

wine

jade mix

COTTON CATS p. 108
A 42 (47, 50)cm chest
B 54 (57, 59)cm length

pale grey

écru

deep pink

bluebell

brown

black

WAISTCOAT
A 49cm chest
B 60cm length

pale grey mix

white

black

wine

jade mix

All you really need for plain knitting are straight needles and yarn. However, the additional accessories shown here can come in handy. For instance, when knitting in the round, use either a set of double-pointed needles or a circular needle. Special cable needles are useful for cable work. To keep unrequired stitches and yarn separate, use stitch holders and yarn bobbins, and keep track of rows and stitches with a counter. Scissors, pins, blunt-ended needles and a crochet hook are helpful in finishing off and making up. You can enjoy finding unique buttons to give the finished garment that special touch.

1

2

3

4

5

2mm

2¼mm

2¾mm

3mm

3¼mm

3¾mm

4mm

8 4

KNITTING KNOW-HOW

Key
1 Stitch holder
2 Cable needles
3 Stitch and row counter
4 Circular needle
5 Double-pointed needles
6 Tape measure
7 Crochet hook
8 Buttons
9 Pins
10 Scissors
11 Wool needles
12 Yarn bobbins

BASIC TECHNIQUES

The information on the following pages will tell you all you need to know to make the sweaters in the book as well as helping you to design your own patterns.

The instructions are written and illustrated for right-handed knitters. If you are left-handed, reverse any instructions for left and right, or prop the book up in front of a mirror and follow the diagrams in reverse.

CASTING ON

When you begin to work on a pattern, placing the first row of stitches on the needles is known as "casting on". All further rows are worked into these initial loops. Casting on can be done in a number of ways, but when you are casting on to work a welt in twisted rib, it is best to cast on into the back of the stitch.

A slip loop is the first stitch to be made and is the foundation for all the subsequent stitches.

MAKING A SLIP LOOP

1 Wrap the yarn twice around two fingers.

2 With the knitting needle, pull a loop through the twisted yarn on the fingers.

3 Pull both ends of yarn to tighten the slip loop.

CASTING ON WITH TWO NEEDLES

1 With the slip loop on your left-hand needle, insert your right-hand needle through the loop from front to back.

2 Bring the yarn under and over your right-hand needle.

3 Draw up the yarn through the slip loop to make a stitch.

4 Place the stitch on the left-hand needle*. Continue to make more stitches in the same way, drawing the yarn through the last stitch on your left-hand needle.

CASTING ON WITH ONE NEEDLE

1 Hold the needle with the slip loop in the right hand. Wrap the working end of the yarn around the left thumb and hold it in the left palm, ready to begin casting on.

2 Put the needle through the yarn behind the thumb. Slip the thumb out of the yarn and pull the working end of the yarn to secure the new stitch.

3 Repeat these steps until the required number of stitches has been cast on.

WINDING WOOL

To form a ball with the working end on top, unwrap yarn from a hank and wind tightly over three fingers. Remove the coils, change the position and continue winding to form a ball.

CASTING ON INTO THE BACK OF THE STITCH

1 Begin by following steps 1 to 4 of casting on with two needles as far as the asterisk. Put the right-hand needle between the slip loop and the first stitch.

2 Wrap the working yarn under and over the right-hand needle.

3 Draw the right-hand needle through to form a new stitch.

4 Place the new stitch on the left-hand needle. Continue until the required number of stitches has been cast on.

HOLDING NEEDLES AND YARN

The way in which you hold your knitting will affect the tension and evenness of the fabric. Threading the working end of the yarn through the fingers not only makes knitting faster, but also produces a firm, even result.

Holding yarn in the right hand

With the working yarn in your right hand, use the right forefinger to wrap the yarn over the needles.

Threading the yarn

Place the working yarn through the fingers of your left hand in either of the ways shown above.

Holding yarn in the left hand

With the working yarn in your left hand, use the left forefinger to position the yarn while you move the right needle to encircle the yarn to form a new loop.

Threading the yarn

Place the working yarn through the fingers of your right hand in either of the ways shown above.

CASTING OFF

When you end a piece of knitting, such as a sleeve, or part of a piece of knitting, such as up to the neck, you must secure all the stitches by "casting off". This is preferably done on a knit row but you can employ the same technique on a purl row. The stitches, whether knit or purl, should be made loosely. With ribbing, you must follow the pattern, and cast off in both knit and purl.

In knit stitch

1 Knit the first two stitches and insert the tip of your left-hand needle through the first stitch.

2 Lift the first stitch over the second stitch and discard it. Knit the next stitch and continue to lift the first stitch over the second stitch to the end of the row. Be careful not to knit too tightly. For the last stitch, cut your yarn, slip the end through the stitch and pull the yarn tight to fasten off securely.

In purl stitch

Purl the first two (and all subsequent) stitches and continue as for knit stitch above.

BASIC STITCHES

Knit stitch and purl stitch are the two basic knitting stitches. When every row is knitted back and forth on two needles, garter stitch is formed. When one row is knitted and the next purled, stocking stitch is formed (*see overleaf*).

KNIT STITCH (k)

1 With the yarn at the back, insert your right-hand needle from front to back into the first stitch on your left-hand needle.

2 Bring your working yarn under and over the point of your right-hand needle.

3 Draw a loop through and slide the first stitch off your left-hand needle while the new stitch is retained on your right-hand needle. Continue in this way to the end of the row.

4 To knit the next row, turn the work around so that the back is facing you and the worked stitches are held on the needle in your left hand. Proceed to make stitches as above, with the initially empty needle held in your right hand.

PURL STITCH (p)

1 With the yarn at the front, insert your right-hand needle from back to front into the first stitch on your left-hand needle.

2 Bring your working yarn over and around the point of your right-hand needle.

3 Draw a loop through and slide the first stitch off your left-hand needle while the new stitch is retained on your right-hand needle. Continue in this way to the end of the row.

4 To purl the next row, turn the work around so that the back is facing you and the worked stitches are held on the needle in your left hand. Proceed to make stitches as above, with the initially empty needle held in your right hand.

TENSION

Before starting to **make any** garment you must make a tension sample in order to measure stitch gauge. You should do this in order to check your individual control of the yarn against the pattern you are following, so that the desired measurements are the same as in the pattern. It is also imperative to do this when you are planning a design of your own, or adapting one.

The stitch gauge, or tension, is always given at the beginning of a pattern. It is written as the number of stitches, and the number of rows in a particular pattern, e.g. stocking stitch, to a specified size, such as 10cm, using the yarn and needles called for in the pattern. An example is 32 sts and 32 rows to 10cm over Fair Isle pattern on 4mm needles.

A variation in tension within a garment will result in an uneven appearance. By knitting the required number of stitches and rows, your sample will reveal whether the yarn and needles you are using will make up into the size and shape you require. When working your tension sample, you must take into account the pattern and the method of carrying yarns across the back of the work (see p. 137).

The paper band around your ball of wool provides important information regarding stitch gauge. The one shown above gives metric and US crochet hook and needle sizes and the ideal tension sample. It is advisable to consult the ball band if the yarn you are using is different from that specified in the pattern.

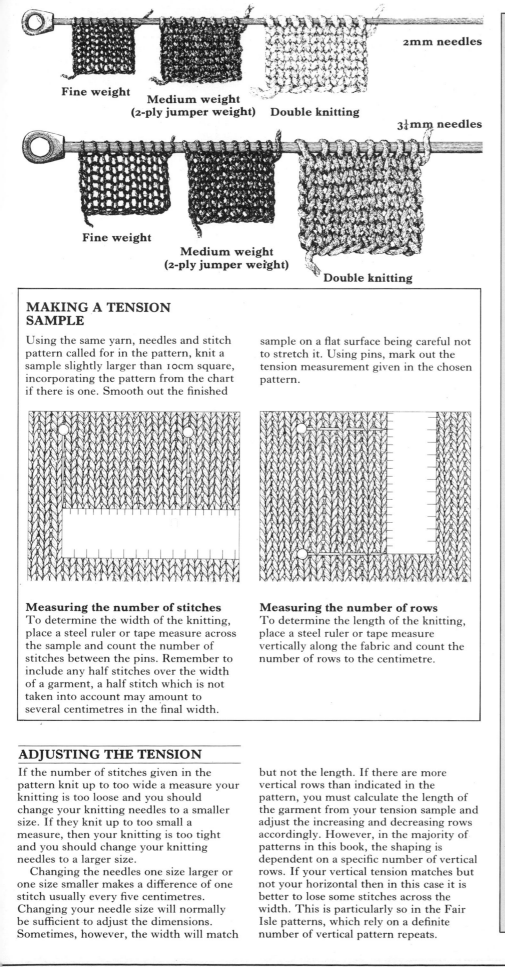

Fine weight

Medium weight
(2-ply jumper weight)   Double knitting

2mm needles

Fine weight

Medium weight
(2-ply jumper weight)

Double knitting

3¼mm needles

MAKING A TENSION SAMPLE

Using the same yarn, needles and stitch pattern called for in the pattern, knit a sample slightly larger than 10cm square, incorporating the pattern from the chart if there is one. Smooth out the finished sample on a flat surface being careful not to stretch it. Using pins, mark out the tension measurement given in the chosen pattern.

Measuring the number of stitches
To determine the width of the knitting, place a steel ruler or tape measure across the sample and count the number of stitches between the pins. Remember to include any half stitches over the width of a garment, a half stitch which is not taken into account may amount to several centimetres in the final width.

Measuring the number of rows
To determine the length of the knitting, place a steel ruler or tape measure vertically along the fabric and count the number of rows to the centimetre.

ADJUSTING THE TENSION

If the number of stitches given in the pattern knit up to too wide a measure your knitting is too loose and you should change your knitting needles to a smaller size. If they knit up to too small a measure, then your knitting is too tight and you should change your knitting needles to a larger size.

Changing the needles one size larger or one size smaller makes a difference of one stitch usually every five centimetres. Changing your needle size will normally be sufficient to adjust the dimensions. Sometimes, however, the width will match

but not the length. If there are more vertical rows than indicated in the pattern, you must calculate the length of the garment from your tension sample and adjust the increasing and decreasing rows accordingly. However, in the majority of patterns in this book, the shaping is dependent on a specific number of vertical rows. If your vertical tension matches but not your horizontal then in this case it is better to lose some stitches across the width. This is particularly so in the Fair Isle patterns, which rely on a definite number of vertical pattern repeats.

MEASUREMENTS

Before you knit up any garment make sure the measurements given in the pattern are suitable for you. The sizes of the sweaters in this book are all given on pp. 116–123. The measurements included are: length of sweater, length of underarm seams and chest/bust width. The chest/bust sizes given in the patterns are the sizes the sweaters are designed to fit, not the actual size of the sweaters.

Taking measurements

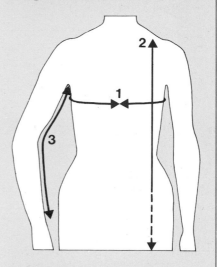

1 **Chest/bust** Measure around the fullest part.

2 **Length** Measure from the nape of the neck to the bottom of the sweater.

3 **Sleeve** Measure from the armpit to the wrist.

An easy way of checking whether the length of the sleeve and length of sweater are suitable for you, is to measure an existing sweater and compare the given measurements with that.

Hats
To calculate the minimum size needed for a hat or cap, measure around the head at the widest part to obtain the circumference. Measure across the top of the head from ear tip to ear tip and divide by two to obtain the minimum length necessary from the crown to the headband edge.

GARTER STITCH

Knitting or purling every row back and forth on two needles produces garter stitch. This stitch is used to separate bands of pattern in the sweaters.

STOCKING STITCH (st st)

Knitting the first and every odd row and purling the second and every even row produces stocking stitch when using two needles. Knitting every row produces stocking stitch when working in the round (see p. 133).

TURKISH STITCH

Turkish stitch is a decorative stitch used to break up rows of pattern horizontally. It features on the Rose cardigan, the Wallflower boat neck sweater and the Sweetpea camisole. It is a much more open stitch than stocking stitch and forms a mesh pattern which is the same on both sides of the garment. Knit the first stitch in the row and then continue as follows:

1 Bring the wool forward.

RIBBING

A combination of knit and purl stitches in the same row is known as ribbing. Ribbing is used on sleeve and body edges to form a neat stretchable finish. It is usually worked on smaller needles than

1 Knit into the back of the first and every knit stitch.

2 Slip the next stitch on to your right-hand needle.

3 Knit the next stitch.

4 Pass the slipped stitch over the knit stitch. Repeat this sequence to the last stitch in the row. Knit the last stitch.

the body of the garment. In this book twisted rib is used as this gives a tighter, neater finish. It is worked in almost the same way as ordinary rib, except that the right-hand needle is put into the *back* of the knit stitch instead of the front.

2 Purl in the ordinary way. Work back across the following rows in the same way, beginning every row with a knit stitch.

DROPPED STITCHES

Occasionally, a stitch may fall off your needle. This is especially likely if you leave off working in the middle of a row.

Picking up a dropped knit stitch

1 Pick up both the stitch and strand on your right-hand needle, inserting the needle from front to back.

2 Insert your left-hand needle through the stitch only, from back to front. With your right-hand needle only, pull the strand through the stitch to make the extra stitch. (Drop the stitch from your left-hand needle.)

3 Transfer the re-formed stitch back to your left-hand needle, so that it untwists and faces the correct way. It is now ready for knitting again.

Picking up a dropped purl stitch

1 Pick up both the stitch and strand on your right-hand needle, inserting the needle from back to front.

2 Insert your left-hand needle through the stitch only, from front to back. With your right-hand needle only, pull the strand through the stitch to make the extra stitch. (Drop the stitch from your left-hand needle.)

3 Transfer the re-formed stitch back to your left-hand needle, so that it untwists and faces the correct way. It is now ready for purling again.

UNPICKING MISTAKES

Holding the stitch on your right-hand needle insert your left-hand needle into the row below and undo the stitch. Transfer the stitch back to your right-hand needle and repeat undoing until the error has been reached. Correct stitch as if it had been a ladder, see right.

LADDERS

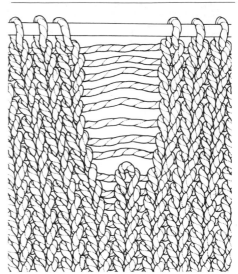

If a dropped stitch is left, it can unravel downwards and form a "ladder". In such a case it is easiest to use a crochet hook to pick up the stitches in pattern although you can try it with your needles. If you make a mistake in your knitting, you may have to "unpick" a stitch, in which case a ladder may result. Pick up one dropped stitch at a time, securing any others with a safety pin to prevent further unraveling.

Correcting a knit ladder

Insert a crochet hook through the front of the dropped stitch. Hook up one strand and pull it through the stitch to form a new stitch one row up. Continue in this way to the top of the ladder then continue in pattern.

Correcting a purl ladder

Insert a crochet hook through the back of the dropped stitch. Hook up one strand and pull it through the stitch to form a new stitch one row up. Continue to re-insert hook to make stitches until you reach the top of the ladder.

READING THE CHARTS

Nearly all the designs in this book are based on Fair Isle or figurative patterns, so reading the charts correctly is essential to the successful working of the patterns. As you will see, different designs stretch over a different number of stitches in a row, but overall the number of stitches and the number of rows in the basic block of the design must relate to the proportions of the finished garment. However, although the pattern might fit perfectly with a garment in a certain size, when the size is increased or decreased, a few extra stitches may need to be worked in the pattern at the beginning and end of rows to achieve the correct number of stitches required by that particular size. Since many of the patterns carry instructions for working the pattern charts in a number of sizes, it is necessary to pick up the design in different places on the chart to accommodate the individual sizes.

The pattern charts are read from right to left on knit rows and from left to right on purl rows. This means that for your first row you start with the stitch at the bottom right-hand corner and work across to the bottom left-hand corner. The chart is always read upwards from bottom to top. The rows are numbered on the left and right-hand sides of the charts; odd (knit) rows are marked on the right and even (purl) rows are marked on the left. The stitches are numbered in italics across the bottom of the chart and are numbered as for working knit rows.

WORKING A SIMPLE CHART

Given right is an example of a chart for a sweater based on a pattern which is made up of a certain number of stitches which, when multiplied, fit exactly into the width of the sweater for both sizes given. This is the simplest way of working a pattern across the rows. The instructions for this chart would read as follows (instructions in brackets are for the larger size):

Repeat the 25 pattern stitches 6 (7) times across the row.

This means that you start at stitch *1* on row 1, and knit across from right to left until you have worked stitch *25*. It is then necessary to repeat the pattern chart another five (six) times across to complete the row. Having worked stitch *25*, you therefore start at *1* again and work across to *25*, five (six) times in all. You will then have completed your first knit row. (Weave the different coloured yarns in, or strand them as you introduce new colours, see p. 137.) Your next row, row 2, will be a purl row. Purl rows are worked in *reverse,* which means that you start with stitch *25* and work back across to stitch *1*. You will then repeat stitches *25–1,* five (six) more times to complete the row. Continue working the pattern in this way until you have completed the number of rows in the chart (68 in this case). You have now completed the first working of the pattern chart. To achieve the required length you will probably need to repeat the pattern chart once, twice or several times. This means that when you have worked row 68, you go back to row 1 at the bottom of the chart, and work up the chart again in the same way.

purl rows

knit rows

25
Start p rows here (all sizes)

1
Start k rows here (all sizes)

25 pattern sts

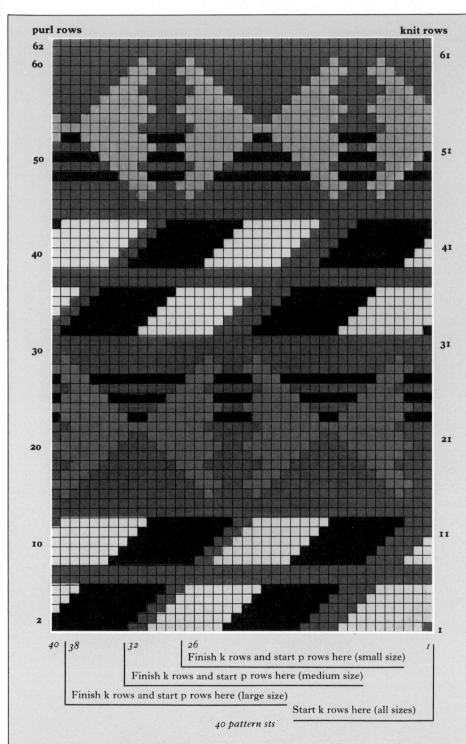

purl rows

knit rows

62
60
50
40
30
20
10
2

61
51
41
31
21
11
1

40 38   32   26   1

Finish k rows and start p rows here (small size)

Finish k rows and start p rows here (medium size)

Finish k rows and start p rows here (large size)

Start k rows here (all sizes)

40 pattern sts

MORE COMPLEX CHARTS

Sometimes a pattern chart will not fit exactly into the width of a sweater, or, when sized up or down, the proportions of the sweater no longer correspond exactly with the proportions of the chart. To repeat the pattern across the rows in this instance it is necessary to work an extra part of the chart to complete the row. This may also happen when working other parts of the sweater, such as the sleeves so, although a front or back might start with the basic number of pattern stitches, the sleeves might need to start

in a different place on the chart. For example, a pattern which contains three sizes is written and worked like this: Work the pattern across knit rows as follows: *for the small size*, work sts *1–40* once, then work sts *1–26* once; *for the medium size*, work sts *1–40* once, then work sts *1–32* once; *for the large size*, work sts *1–40* once, then work sts *1–38* once. Work purl rows in reverse (i.e. work *26–1* once, then *40–1* once for the small size and so on).

TAKING EXTRA STITCHES INTO THE PATTERN

When you are working a shaped piece such as a sleeve, the side edges are shaped as you progress. Normally the stitches are increased at the side edge, but the extra stitches so made must be taken into the pattern. To do this you treat the new stitch in the same way as you would work the next stitch in the row. So if, for example, your row finished with stitch *16* of a pattern comprising *16* basic pattern stitches, and you increased on stitch *16*, you would work the new stitch in the same way as stitch *1*.

REPEATING THE PATTERN CHART UP THE GARMENT

The number of times the pattern chart is repeated as you work up the garment is referred to as so many workings of the pattern chart. When you work through the pattern you will see that the number of rows worked is related to the approximate length of the work at that point, and this measurement is dependent on the tension of your knitting. If you are not working at the required tension you will find that the measurements and the number of rows do not tally.

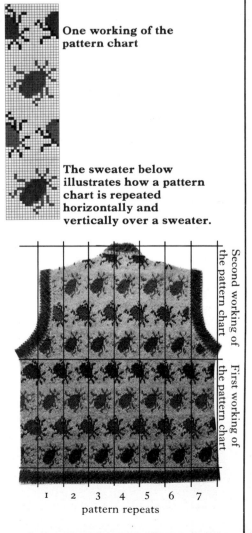

One working of the pattern chart

The sweater below illustrates how a pattern chart is repeated horizontally and vertically over a sweater.

Second working of the pattern chart

First working of the pattern chart

1 2 3 4 5 6 7

pattern repeats

WORKING WITH MORE THAN ONE COLOUR

Since most of Sasha's designs are multi-coloured, there are several techniques you need to know about in order to successfully complete one of these sweaters. When more than one colour is being used in a row, the yarn that is not being used has to be carried across the back of the knitting ready to be used when called for by the chart. The way in which this is done can greatly influence the tension of the knitting and so it must be done correctly. There are various ways of joining in yarns and carrying yarns across, and different patterns and different parts of a sweater will require different methods, these different methods are all explained below. Yarn bobbins can be used to help keep the different yarns separate, or when working a block of colour.

ADDING NEW YARN IN THE MIDDLE OF A ROW

This method is not recommended when a colour is repeated right across the row and up several rows. It is only suitable for working a small area of stitches in one colour. If you join in the yarn for each block of colour in a figurative pattern you will find that your tension is completely thrown and a much larger garment results, with small holes where each of the yarns has been added.

1 Insert your right-hand needle through the first stitch on your left-hand needle. Wrap the new yarn over, and knit (or purl) the stitch with the new yarn. Leave the old yarn at the back of the work.

Make the back of your work as neat as possible, darning in ends of yarn

2 Knit (or purl) the next two stitches using the double length of new yarn.

ADDING NEW YARN AT THE BEGINNING OF A ROW

This is the way in which you should join in the yarn if you are working striped rib, either for the welts and cuffs or when working an entire back in striped rib. When you work with the additional colours it is best to carry the yarns not in use up the sides of the work until they are required again. When you have finished using a particular colour of yarn, darn the end of the yarn neatly into the edge or the back of the work.

2 Leaving the old yarn at the back, knit (or purl) the next two stitches using the double length of the new yarn.

1 Insert right-hand needle through first stitch on left-hand needle and wrap the old, and then the new yarn over it. Knit (or purl) the stitch using both yarns.

3 Discard the short end of the new yarn and continue to knit as usual. On the following row treat the three double stitches as single stitches.

3 Discard the short end of the new yarn and continue to knit as usual. On the following row, treat the two double stitches as single stitches.

CARRYING YARN ACROSS THE BACK OF THE WORK

The two following methods – stranding and weaving – are the most suitable for carrying the different colours across the rows, and both avoid holes appearing as you introduce a new colour. Choose the method which you feel most comfortable with. Weaving is the most effective, as it leaves the back of the work neat and hard-wearing, whereas stranding leaves loose yarns at the back which are easily pulled. Whether stranding or weaving, try to keep your tension as close as you can to the tension given in the pattern. You may find you prefer to mix the two techniques, stranding those yarns which appear infrequently and weaving those which recur often. As a general guide, strand yarn over two to five stitches, weave yarn when it has to be carried over more than five stitches.

STRANDING YARN

In a knit row
With both yarns at the back of the work, knit the required number of stitches with yarn A (in this case two), and then drop it to the back. Pick up yarn B and knit the required number of stitches and then drop it to the back. Both yarns should be stranded loosely along the back of the work.

In a purl row
With both yarns at the front of the work, purl the required number of stitches with yarn A (in this case two), and then drop it. Pick up yarn B and purl the required number of stitches and then drop it. Both yarns should be stranded loosely along the front (side facing you).

WEAVING YARN

In a knit row

1 Hold yarn A in your right hand and yarn B in your left hand to the back of the work.

2 Knit one stitch with yarn A and, at the same time, bring yarn B below yarn A. When yarn B is being used weave yarn A as above.

In a purl row

1 Hold yarn A in your right hand and yarn B in your left hand to the front of the work.

2 Purl one stitch with yarn A but this time bring yarn B below yarn A. When yarn B is being used, weave yarn A as above.

CHECKING YOUR TECHNIQUE

To prevent the different yarns getting tangled, the strands must be caught up in the back of the work, but not so as they interfere with the pattern or produce undesired effects.

If you have worked weaving correctly, the yarns will cross evenly and remain at the same depth. A "smocking" effect means that you have pulled the yarns too tightly. It is better for the yarns to be woven too loosely than too tightly.

If you have worked stranding correctly, the yarns will be running evenly across the back of the work at the same tension as the knitting. Puckering indicates that you have pulled the yarns too tightly.

PICKING UP STITCHES AND RIBBING

After working the fronts, back and sleeves, the ribbing for the front bands, armhole bands, pocket tops and neckband should be worked. When a garment has a collar, this is usually knitted after the main body of the sweater has been completed, and sewn on afterwards. K1, p1 twisted rib is used for all these features (see p. 130), and usually it is worked on to a cast-off edge or side selvedge. To do this, stitches have to be picked up from these edges, and the ribbing then worked on these newly picked up stitches.

Sometimes the shoulder seams have to be joined before picking up and ribbing stitches. For instructions on seams see right.

PICKING UP STITCHES

Always pick up stitches with the right side of the work facing you. Where you start on a garment will depend on which piece of the garment you are working on, because you always work from right to left. If, for example, you are picking up stitches along the right front opening edge of a waistcoat, start at the hem edge for the right front opening edge and at the centre-back of the neck for the left front opening edge. The number of stitches you pick up does not necessarily correspond with the number of rows in the edge along which you are picking up the stitches. The number of buttonholes needed and the appropriate number of stitches between them will dictate the number of stitches down a front opening edge. For a stronger, neater finish, pick up stitches from the last line of knitting before the cast-off edge or side selvedge.

Use this method of picking up stitches for buttonhole and button bands, armhole bands, pocket tops and linings, and neckbands. Once you have picked up the stitches, work the bands in k1, p1 twisted rib in the same way as the welts. Sometimes a contrasting coloured yarn is joined in for the last row of rib. In this case, cast off in rib in this colour yarn.

When you encounter stitches which have been left on a spare needle or stitch holder, merely knit these in as you put them on the needle. Then work in rib along with all other picked up stitches.

1 Place your needle through the work and bring the yarn round as if knitting the stitch.

2 Pull the yarn through the stitch from the main work, to make a stitch on the needle.

3 Continue making stitches in this way, always placing the needle into a firm stitch on the main piece of work, until you have the correct amount on the needle. Sew the ends of the yarn in when the band is complete.

SELVEDGES

The sides of a piece of knitting are also known as selvedges. Special care must be taken to ensure that these are kept straight. There are various ways of working edges, but for the purposes of this book a stocking stitch is best. The first and last stitches must be firmly made, particularly on front opening edges and armhole edges, since stitches will be picked up from these later. All knit row stitches are knitted and all purl row stitches are purled.

BUTTONHOLE BANDS

Join the front to the back at the shoulder seams. Work the required number of rows of twisted rib as given in the pattern, after picking up the stitches. The first edge of the buttonhole is usually made in a right-side row. Normally the buttonhole occupies 3 stitches, so if you need to calculate the number of stitches required between buttonholes, take this into account. In these patterns the positions of the buttonholes are already worked out. Rib the required number of stitches in the row in the usual way, then cast off three stitches, then rib the number of stitches required between this and the next buttonhole edge, and so on, until you have cast off the correct number of edges for the buttonholes. On the next row, rib back in the same way as before, but each time you reach the cast-off edge in the previous row, cast on 3 stitches directly over this cast-off edge. Continue in rib for the required number of rows, then cast off.

Wrong side of buttonhole band

NECKBANDS

Stitches around the neck can be picked up and worked either in the round, using four double pointed needles, or a circular needle, or they can be picked up in the same way as buttonhole bands using two needles, and the two ends of ribbing can then be joined together with a flat seam. If using two needles you will have to join the front to the back at one shoulder. If working in the round, join both shoulder seams. (See p. 133 for working in the round.) Complete the band in the same way as all other bands.

POCKETS

Pockets are worked in either of two ways in this book. Either the lower edge of the pocket opening is cast off, or these stitches are transferred to a spare needle or stitch holder. Where they have been cast off the appropriate number of stitches must be picked up across this edge. The pocket top is then worked in rib as before. Where the stitches are left on a spare needle, merely rib them from the spare needle.

Similarly, pocket linings are either worked on a cast-on edge directly over the cast-off edge, or they are incorporated in the main working of the fronts. If the stitches are picked up from a cast-on edge, pick up in the usual way, but work the lining in stocking stitch, not rib.

MAKING UP

Many of the sweaters in this book are based on six basic shapes, and therefore share many of the same methods of making up. Given overleaf are the basic ways of making up a waistcoat, a gilet, a crew neck sweater, a boat neck sweater, a V-neck cardigan and a round neck cardigan. Full instructions are given with each pattern for camisoles, peplum jackets, hats and legwarmers. Before making up, you may wish to block the individual pieces of knitting, see right.

SEAMS

There are several different methods for joining pieces of knitting together. The following techniques are suitable for use with the sweaters in this book. Use yarn to match the main or background colour of the sweater.

RIDGED EDGE-TO-EDGE SEAM

Use this seam for sleeve seams, shoulder seams and side seams. Since it is worked from the right side it is easy to match patterns. It forms a visible seam ridge on the inside, but gives a neater finish on the right side than the flat edge-to-edge seam.

Place the pieces to be joined, edge-to-edge, right side up. Match the pieces carefully, row for row and stitch for stitch. Using the main yarn, make the seam from the right side in the same way

as the flat edge-to-edge seam, but do not sew into the edge stitches, instead make the seam one stitch in from the edge, so that a ridge forms on the inside of the garment.

FLAT EDGE-TO-EDGE SEAM

The ends of front bands, neckbands and armhole bands should be joined with this seam since it gives a flat finish. It is worked from the right side.

Place the pieces to be joined edge-to-edge, right side up. Match the pieces carefully, row for row and stitch for stitch. Using the main yarn, sew the edge stitches of both pieces together so that the edges meet.

BACKSTITCH SEAM

Backstitched seams are made from the wrong side, so carefully pin the seams first to make sure the patterns match on the right side.

FINISHING TECHNIQUES

Before pattern pieces are joined up, they are usually blocked and pressed to ensure a good fit. It's always a good idea to check the yarn band for any special instructions. The pieces are blocked when dry and are pressed with a damp cloth.

Garment pieces may need blocking, or putting into shape, before they can be joined up. Cover a table with a folded blanket and a sheet. Lay the knitting the wrong side up on the sheet. Using rustless pins pin the knitting by its edges to the blanket, gently pulling it into shape and to the correct measurements, making sure that the rows run in straight lines. Be careful not to stretch or distort the fabric since if you do so, during use it will resume its original size and shape.

Blocking

After blocking, the garment pieces are usually pressed in position. Use a warm iron and a clean, absorbent, damp cloth on wool. Lay the iron on the fabric and lift up, do not move it over the surface. Do not press too heavily as this will flatten the knitting. Do not remove any of the pins until the piece as cooled and dried completely.

Raised and embossed patterns should be pressed under a damp cloth, but remove the pins and adjust the fabric while it is still hot to avoid the patterns being flattened.

Avoid pressing ribbing and fancy stitches, such as Turkish stitch, as they will lose their elasticity.

Pressing

ABBREVIATIONS

beg	beginning
dec	decrease
foll	following
garter st	knit or purl every row
g	gram
inc	increase
k	knit
k2 tog	knit two stitches together
moss st	k1, p1 to end; next row p1, k1 to end
()	repeat all the instructions between brackets as many times as indicated
psso	pass slip stitch over
p	purl
rep from *	repeat all the instructions that follow asterisk
sl	slip
st	stitch
st st	stocking stitch
tog	together
Turkish st	k1, *yfwd, sl 1, k1, psso; repeat from *
turn	turn the work around at the point indicated, before the end of a row
up 1 k	insert needle from front to back into loop of st below next one to be knitted, knit loop, then knit next st on left hand needle
up 1 p	insert needle from back to front into top of st below next one to be knitted, purl this loop, then purl next st on left hand needle
up 1 p k	insert needle from back to front into top of st below next st to be knitted, purl this loop, then knit next st on left hand needle
yfwd	yarn forward

CENTIMETRES/INCHES CONVERSION CHART

cm	in	cm	in
1	½	21	8¼
2	¾	22	8¾
3	1¼	23	9
4	1½	24	9½
5	2	25	9¾
6	2¼	26	10¼
7	2¾	27	10¾
8	3¼	28	11
9	3½	29	11½
10	4	30	11¾
11	4¼	31	12¼
12	4¾	32	12½
13	5	33	13
14	5½	34	13½
15	6	35	13¾
16	6¼	36	14¼
17	6¾	37	14½
18	7	38	15
19	7½	39	15¼
20	7¾	40	15¾

◄ Please note that these conversions are approximate to the nearest ¼ inch.

GRAMS/OUNCES CONVERSION CHART

grams	ounces
25	1
50	1¾
75	2¾
100	3½
125	4½
150	5¼
175	6¼
200	7
225	8
250	8¾
275	9¾
300	10½
325	11½
350	12¼
375	13¼
400	14
425	15
450	15¾

◄ Please note that these conversions are approximate. One ounce = approximately 28.35 grams.

KNITTING NEEDLES CONVERSION CHART

Metric (mm)	2¼	2¾	3	3¼	3¾	4
English	13	12	11	10	9	8
U.S.	0	1	2	3	4	5

SASHA KAGAN YARN SERVICE

Packs of sufficient yarn for knitting each of the sweaters in this book are available by mail order. Send for details, enclosing a S.A.E. to:
Sasha Kagan Knitwear (yarn supplies)
Llanidloes
Powys
Wales SY18 6AD
Sasha Kagan is also able to supply many of these sweaters knitted up as special orders. Send for details to the above address, quoting **Sweater Service.**
Note: While Sasha's patterns are long-standing, individual yarn shades may go out of stock in time. She is willing to suggest and/or supply alternative yarns and colourways.

YARN INFORMATION

Alternatively 2-ply jumper weight Shetland yarn can be ordered directly from the manufacturers. Write for a shade card to:
Jamieson & Smith (Shetland Wool Brokers) Ltd
90 North Road
Lerwick
Shetland Isles, ZE1 0PQ

The cotton yarn used for these sweaters is Mayflower cotton 8, which is distributed by Aero Needles Group. For a list of stockists write to:
Aero Needles Group Ltd
Box No 2
Edward Street
Redditch
Worcestershire B97 6HB
This is a fine cotton and knits up in the same way as 4-ply (medium weight) yarn. Twilleys also manufacture a similar cotton yarn.

The mohair yarn used was manufactured by Lister and the lurex yarn by Twilleys.

WASHING KNITWEAR

Always use a mild soap, preferably one especially designed for knitwear, and warm water. Before washing a brightly-coloured garment, check that it is colour-fast by dipping a small piece of it into the soapy water. Press it out in a white cloth. If it leaves a stain, wash in cold water.

1 Always squeeze the suds into the garment gently and do not rub or felting will occur. Don't leave the garment to soak, but rinse and remove quickly. Make certain the rinse water is clear before removing the garment. You can add fabric softener to the last rinse if you wish.

2 Place the garment in a thick towel, white if possible, and roll both up. You can place extra towels on top of the garment for extra absorption if you like before rolling up. Press the roll with your hands or "hammer" it with your fists to remove as much water as possible. You can repeat this with another towel if the garment is still very wet, or to facilitate drying.

3 Finish drying the garment by laying it out flat on another clean towel, away from direct heat. Make sure the knitting is correctly shaped. Store the garment in a drawer; never hang it up as it can be easily pulled out of shape.

RE-USING YARN

If you are unpicking a made-up garment, undo the seams first and then locate the last cast-off stitch. Start here to unravel the knitting, winding it around the back of a chair to keep the yarn from getting tangled or stretched, and to facilitate washing. Fasten the hank at two ends; catch the end of the yarn in one of the ties. Hand wash then rewind yarn into loose balls when dry.

ACKNOWLEDGEMENTS

The author and publishers would like to thank the following people
for their help in producing this book:

Illustrators
Elaine Anderson
Lindsay Blow
John Hutchinson
Edwina Keene
Coral Mula

Photographers
Paul Fletcher
Colin Molyneux
Ian O'Leary
Colin Thomas

Reproduction
Reprocolor International

Typesetters
Chambers Wallace

Melanie Miller, Debra Grayson and Grail Dorling for
their editorial help; Workshop Clothing Ltd for lending
many of the shirts and skirts used in the photographs;
Neal Street East shop for Oriental goods; Monsoon for
accessories. We are also extremely grateful to the following
for kindly lending us props for the photographs: Bayat van
Dunk, Jubilee Market; Boosey & Hawkes Ltd; Dutch
Dairy Bureau; Freed of London; Lucy Goffin; Clare
Hart; The Hat Shop; London Graphic Centre; David
Mellor; Stuart Mooney, Jubilee Market; Moss Bros Ltd;
Mulberry Co. (Design) Ltd; Naturally British, British
Handmade Crafts; Oasis Trading Ltd; Geraldine
St. Aubin Hubbard; The Scotch House; Scotts of Camden
Town; Souleiado Ltd, French Provencale Fabrics;
Talisman; Caroline Thomas; Tiger, Tiger (King's Road)
Ltd; Paul Wu; Wallis; Laura Ashley; Lumiere; Dolcis; Sacha;
Visuals; Ally Capellino; Warehouse and Adrien Mann.